moderncountry

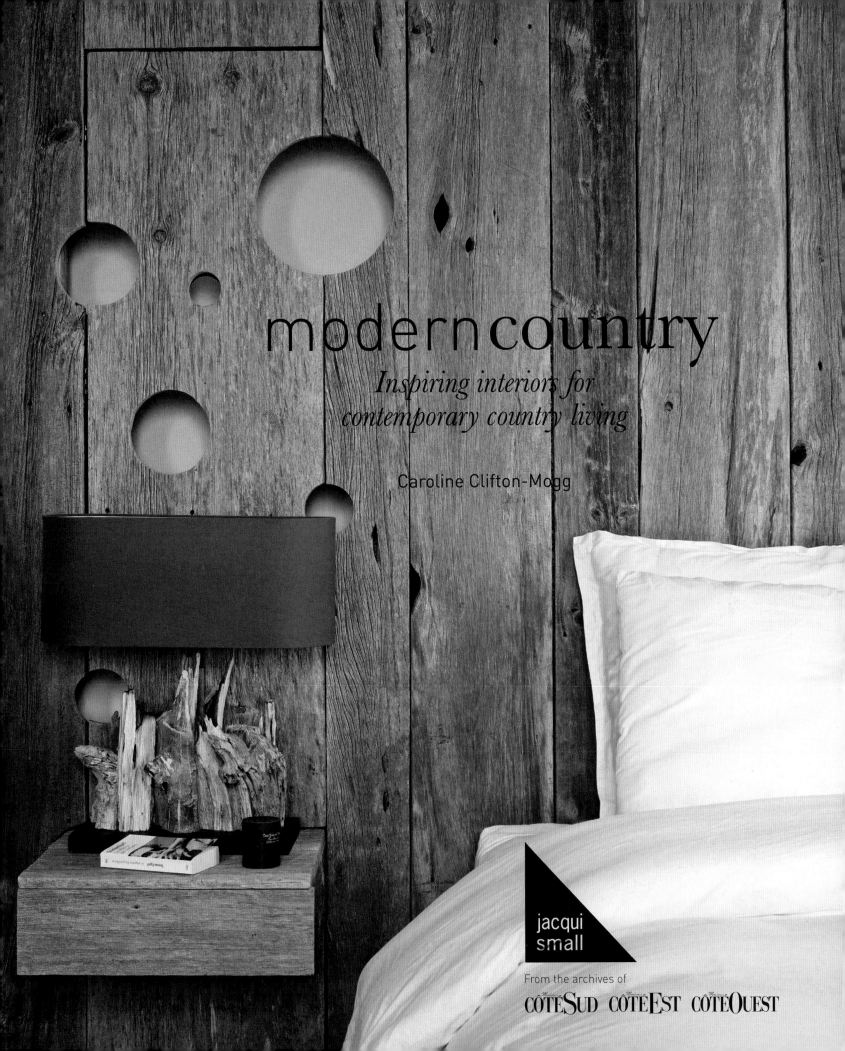

moderncountry

*Inspiring interiors for
contemporary country living*

Caroline Clifton-Mogg

jacqui
small

From the archives of
CÔTÉSUD CÔTÉEST CÔTÉOUEST

First published in 2014 by
Jacqui Small LLP
An imprint of Aurum Press
74–77 White Lion Street
London N1 9PF

Text copyright © 2014 Caroline Clifton-Mogg
Photography copyright © 2014 Groupe Express-Roularta
Design and layout copyright © 2014 Jacqui Small

Publisher: Jacqui Small
Associate Publisher: Joanna Copestick
Managing Editor: Lydia Halliday
Editor: Sian Parkhouse
Designer: Sarah Rock
Production: Maeve Healy

ISBN: 978 1 909342194

A catalogue record for this book is available from the
British Library.

2016 2015 2014
10 9 8 7 6 5 4 3 2 1

Printed in China

Page 1 *White rough-cast walls, bleached
even whiter by the bright hot sun – this is
one of the country ideals that we dream of on
overlong winter days.*

Previous pages left *Modern country dining
can be every bit as sophisticated as modern
city life. The differences are subtle: the
texture of the floors and walls, the style of
the table and chairs, the feeling of ease.*

Previous pages right *Clever ways with
traditional materials are what make the
modern country look; wide old oak boards
are turned into an inner wall with varying
sizes of planks or circles seemingly cut out
at random.*

Right *Comfort is king; in the country, even
the dining room, grand as it is with its drop
chandelier, is made comfortable and relaxing
with the deep-pillowed chaise longue in a
corner – ready for a rest between courses?*

Contents

Introduction

Until well into the nineteenth century, most of mainland Europe was predominantly rural, and the roots of most people were those of the countryside. The geological and natural landscapes that people knew and grew up with were those of woods and pastures, mountains and hills, rivers and lakes. There was a tradition of how life was conducted, and this sense of tradition, even in our speeded-up technological era, is as strong as it always was.

So a modern country style, although emphatically of the twenty-first century, is still based on, and evolved from, that rural tradition, even when that tradition is brought bang up to date. Lightness of living is important – an understanding of the things that make life pleasant, such as family and friends, comfort and ease, food and drink. The houses in Modern Country *reflect these desires and concerns, and throughout the book we can see the inventive and imaginative ideas and solutions that home owners have employed to make their home, large or small, worth living in, whether they have used professional help or gone it alone.*

Whether they are reaching back into the past, standing firmly in the present or looking forwards into the future, and whichever design and architectural route has been taken, one thread that runs through each and every one of these homes is the desire to create a place to live in that is firmly entrenched in the greater countryside.

This page *In this contemporary version of the traditional mountain retreat all the elements are here: beams, a cosy roaring fire, a warm bare-toe rug and comfortable seats. The difference is that it is all presented in an utterly modern way, with clean lines, uncluttered shapes and cool colours.*

Right *We all have our different visions of what the countryside is, but quite aside from specifics, there are certain givens that we seek – fresh, sweet air, natural beauty and light, space to walk and sit and room to just be.*

COUNTRY
LOCATIONS

Close-knit communities

Throughout Europe for hundreds of years daily life has been rural; much of it was passed within relatively small communities, villages and hamlets and small market towns – each part of the greater whole. This is something you still see today in the larger cities, where the life of the quartier *or suburb is of greater interest than that of the life of the city as a whole. And because so many lived off the land, there were and are many houses built in fairly isolated positions – close to the fields that were being worked, the livestock that was being cared for in the mountains or the sea that was the source of fish for food and sale.*

Previous pages *When perfection is already present, there is nothing that can improve it: a traditional chalet with a traditional wooden balcony; a comfortable wooden-slatted chair with cushions and rugs, facing a view of mountains and valleys that defies description.*

Right *An infinity pool, the most magical contemporary version of the swimming pool, designed so that the sea in the distance seems to be almost an extension of the pool. Reflected in the water is a house built in the traditional manner with dry-stone walls.*

Above *A very basic stone shepherd's hut in a perfect Mediterranean pine-wood setting. As a conversion this is perfect – the building has retained its simple structure, and seems to be part of the surrounding landscape.*

Right *Throughout the South of Europe, local stone is used to build steps and terraces in order to work and live on the steep terrain. Here, a set of stone steps is softened by vegetation that is encouraged to grow over the stone edges.*

Far right *A flat rooftop was transformed into an airy terrace with a tiled pergola built from rough beams, the whole so organic that it seems almost like a natural arbour of entwined trees. Hanging swing seats, like floating bee skeps, add to the illusion.*

Transforming buildings

For today's restorers and renovators, turning run-down rural buildings into liveable, manageable homes is far from easy. They may be halfway up a hillside with only a cart track for a road, hidden in the depths of woodland or in the middle of a vineyard with no access to electricity or water. The finished homes, therefore, are the result of much ingenuity and stamina, as well as imagination and sheer staying power – their owners are to be applauded and encouraged, for they give the rest of us hope that if something is worth doing, then the problems can be addressed and the final result will be even more worthwhile.

Left *The olive has always been the symbol of Mediterranean life, and very old specimens such as this one, with its thick-gnarled trunk, living in a whitewashed and stone courtyard, are treasured.*

Below *A whitewashed house with a traditional sloping, shallow Mediterranean roof covered with the equally traditional curved terracotta roof tiles – allegedly moulded over a maiden's thigh or, indeed, a log.*

This page and opposite
Contrasting retreats, both with longed-for and sought-after views. On the one hand, stone steps lead to a garden hideaway that looks through trees to a wide bay with glinting water. On the other hand, the log-stacked walls of a wooden mountain chalet afford a sight of majestic snow-covered mountains, unchanging in form, altered only by the shifting light.

Rural Havens

Since Europe was – and remains, if only in terms of acreage – in large part rural, it follows that in and around every village and town there are pastoral houses and buildings – cottages, farmhouses, manors, shepherds' huts, old stables, barns and dairies.

Some were originally built for human occupation, others designed to house animals or crops, but today these are potential rural retreats, one and all. Interestingly, after two centuries of rural depopulation there has begun a movement, particularly in France over the last ten years, towards moving away from larger towns and back to the countryside to repopulate rural areas. A combination of disillusionment with urban life and the price of housing in urban areas in comparison with rural costs, as well as a general disaffection and disenchantment, has meant that some buyers are restoring, repairing and converting rural buildings and houses out of choice.

So, although this book is about the idea of modern country living, not all the houses featured are modern – indeed, many of the original structures are relatively old and built in the traditional manner. What is modern, though, is the way in which those who have chosen to inhabit these buildings have renovated, altered and decorated them to make them contemporary homes – of their time, but with an understanding and respect for what has gone before.

What is notable is how the best of these new–old homes have been designed in an imaginative and inventive manner that goes beyond the traditional idea of renovation. Seamless, almost invisible extensions have been added, light-filled

Opposite and right *The European countryside is varied and wide. In every country, round every bend is another picture-perfect scene showing rural life at its charming best. From small cottages to large houses, from manicured lawns and clipped topiary to trees heavy with mimosa blossom bending over a grassy corner, every taste can be catered for.*

openings made in what seemed to be impenetrable walls and old and new linked with walkways and terraces. Buildings of great height – industrial barns and the like – have had mezzanine floors and galleries introduced, and constructions once designed to keep out all vagaries of weather, both cold and hot, have been sensitively deconstructed to allow both inside and outside to work as one.

One of the major differences between modern and traditional living is the way that the delineation between rooms has dissolved and softened. Many of the houses here – in particular those that have been renovated and restored – have been completely rearranged inside. In an old farmhouse – particularly in the south – where the living accommodation might have been shared with various livestock, either one end of the lower floor would have been used for human habitation, or the upper floor in its entirety. Obviously, modern ways of living – notably not sharing the accommodation with anything much larger than a cat or dog, or even several of each – have meant that flexibility and imagination can be used to create easy living and sleeping spaces that work whether there is one occupant or twenty. Nearly all the homes here make the kitchen area the heart of the space, more often than not with a commanding table that acts as both the centre of food preparation and as the congenial indoors eating centre. There are rarely separate sitting rooms, rather chairs and sofas set up in places where they will be most used.

The other change between then and now is the emphasis on a connection between inside and outside the house. For home owners today – particularly, but not necessarily, if the house is to be used as a holiday home – it is essential that any outside area, from the smallest terrace or balcony to acres of grounds, is a considered part of the whole. Many of the houses in this book started life as strictly practical, agricultural spaces, whose use was utilitarian rather than for pleasure. There was no need to create outside areas in which to sit in the sun or to eat and drink, or to swim – courtyards were for work or storage; green space, ditto. Even those houses designed originally as dwellings had outside spaces conceived in a different way, and usually for a different purpose – somewhere to grow food or flowers, or even somewhere to walk and sit, but with far less emphasis on an all-day outdoors, leisured life.

Above right *A raised platform surrounding this light-filled house gives an almost transitory appearance to the site. There is a practical advantage though: the wooden terrace will be dry when the surrounding grassland is not.*

Right *The surroundings to this restored rural building have been designed in a suitably rustic manner that blends well with the rough stone walls, wooden shutters and wood-clad upper storey.*

This page *A contemporary house is built on several levels. The principal building is constructed of boards of different widths with horizontal windows carefully positioned to illuminate specific interior areas.*

BRETON STONES

Near Saint-Brieuc in Brittany, an old stone farmhouse has been transformed into a light-filled space, in an unusual and creative way. The house itself had been in the family for over thirty years but unlived in.

It was used rather as a weekend picnic venue, where the whole extended family, generations together – grandparents, children, grandchildren and sons- and daughters-in-law – would all come to eat, ride and be in the Breton countryside. But now it is being transformed by Céline, the youngest of the family, with her husband Marc into a family house as well as three separate holiday cottages – each of which faces onto the old farmyard, now a communal courtyard, with direct access into the countryside beyond.

When converting any old building, particularly an old stone farmhouse built to withstand the often harsh winter weather in this part of France, the introduction of enough natural light is of prime importance. Marc and Céline's solution was a bold one – they sliced into the stone on one side of the house to make

Below *A raised deck or walkway runs round the whole building, connecting everything and giving cohesion to the overall design. Built from rough-hewn, untreated wood, it echoes the solid materials, both old and new, of the farmhouse and the wider landscape.*

This page *A large, stone-framed window cut through the thick old stone wall gives much-needed light and opens up the house, as well as creating a comfortable sitting space against a bosky background.*

a roof-high, iron-framed wall of glass with windows on the upper part and doors that open out into the surrounding wooded landscape. Stone-framed windows were also added where possible – including one in what was the original fireplace hearth. A walkway runs around almost the entire exterior of the house.

Charmingly, and in contrast to the wide open spaces elsewhere, Céline and Marc elected to keep the original enclosed wooden staircase, a reminder of French peasant life for so many centuries. The bedrooms have been equally simply designed, and in the old attics the stone walls have been left partially exposed, except where they have been rendered at floor level with rough cement – as unpolished and as simple as the stonework above.

Above *The necessary and boldest move was to slice through the stone on one side of the house to make a new opening – metal-framed glass doors opening out into the landscape. Metal is a constant theme – inside, sliding metal doors are used to separate the kitchen from the rest of the living space.*

Left *As a charming reminder of the old life of the house, the original narrow staircase, which leads up to the bedroom floor and is lined with wooden board, has been retained.*

Right *A winning combination of the new and the old; there has been no attempt to disguise the fact that this is an old building, but the installation of modern equipment makes it a contemporary kitchen in every sense.*

COUNTRY CONTEMPORARY

One of the dreams of those in search of the perfect rural retreat is that one day,
almost by chance, they will stumble upon a scenic, charming, rustic ruin of a house
(obviously with all its charming, rustic outbuildings), hidden deep in the countryside,
that is just waiting, like Sleeping Beauty, to be awakened with a restorative kiss.

Of course, it doesn't often happen, but when it does it requires more than a single kiss – more practical qualities, such as enormous determination, self-belief and patience are needed in abundance. Here is such a tale.

In the beginning, in the province of Limbourg, close to Hasselt in Belgium, there were the woods and the fields; and, nestling in the middle of the fields, there was a farmhouse, a chicken house and a stable, all of which had been there since the fifteenth century. And it was all very, very dilapidated.

But none of that really matters when you fall in love, and when decorator Dorine Cormans saw the house and its surroundings, she did fall in love and resolved to bring everything back to life. The possibilities were many – the outbuildings were of good proportions and of a scale that meant restoration was viable; many of the original building materials still existed, although in poor repair.

For two years the structural and heavy work went on, two years of digging out earth, of stripping back to the bones and of creating a new architectural structure in the now empty space. The plan was to convert the space into both private quarters and rooms for guests – *chambres d'hôte*.

After those arduous two years, the careful and meticulous planning, the stripping-out, the putting back together again, the project was

Left *An old farmhouse and stables, once dilapidated but picturesque beyond belief, have been renovated in a way that retains every vestige of outward old-world charm while producing a space of peaceful, almost monastic calm.*

This page *In less skilled hands, this room might appear almost sparse, but instead the wide polished floorboards, the simple long table and stretched-out linen-covered sofa make this a quiet, calm – and comfortable – space.*

Below *The breakfast room boasts ceiling-high, metal-framed portes-fenêtres that lead directly onto the garden. The floor is laid in a traditional design of old unpointed bricks, the variation in each brick giving a warm glow to the room.*

Below right *In the hall, the terracotta floor tiles are eighteenth century – reclaimed and restored. They contrast with the limewashed plastered walls and the untreated pale oak doors.*

complete. The finished result is a pleasing and calm space with an almost monastic purity that you sense as soon as you enter.

In the hall, reclaimed eighteenth-century terracotta tiles contrast with the limewash-painted plaster walls and the simple oak staircase. The breakfast room has ceiling-high French windows onto the garden, and a floor that is traditionally laid with unpointed, warm and mellow old bricks. The living room boasts a comfortable linen-covered sofa and chairs and an uncompromisingly modern fireplace that soars from floor to ceiling. The bedrooms are coloured and furnished in the same, almost severe style, and here, as downstairs, there are no paintings – pleasure comes from

the purity of the materials. The severity is tempered, however, by Dorine's choice of accessories – a group of tubular white vases, each with a single bloom; striking pendulum ceiling lights and, everywhere, sculptural ceramics.

Although the colours are neutral, monochrome even, the softness of the finish and the subtlety of the tones give a warmth and depth to every room. Indeed, the whole exercise is a gentle lesson in the art of reinterpreting and presenting the past in a modern yet timeless fashion.

This page *The same contrast of textures and materials is evident in this simple bathroom, where the bowl-shaped basin is set onto a pale oak counter top against a wall of untreated plaster. Beams that have been restored to their natural state add another layer of texture.*

Mountain Retreats

The appeal of the mountain retreat – quite aside from snow-covered mountains, flower-filled alpine meadows and so on – is, for most people, the lure of pure mountain air.

Traditionally, the mountains were where the first convalescent homes and sanatoriums were built – they first became popular in the nineteenth century when doctors prescribed high altitudes and fresh air for tuberculosis sufferers. Even today, one still gets a sense of well-being when breathing the often spicily cold air of the Alps, the Dolomites or the Pyrenees.

European mountain ranges were not appreciated in the same way that they are today until the late eighteenth and early nineteenth centuries. Until then, they were simply seen as difficult and dangerous places through which it was sometimes necessary to travel in rough discomfort and danger – travellers' letters and memoirs resound with the perils of mountain passes, filthy weather and badly sprung coaches. At some point, however, these same travellers realized the grandeur and beauty of the mountains, and from that time paintings and letters extolled the same features they had once disliked.

Below left *The warmth of the seasoned wood boards, the covering of thick snow on the roof and the dark surrounding fir trees all sum up the magic of the mountains.*

Below right *A traditional wooden chalet has been extended and added to in the most sympathetic manner; rather than detracting from the original, the new additions, including a chimney stack, just extend the chalet's simple charms.*

Opposite *A tiny* mazot, *or shepherd's hut, in the middle of an Alpine field has been cleverly made into a perfect mountain retreat; the ground-floor area, usually open to the air, has been enclosed to give welcome additional space.*

And with this new appreciation of the mountains came an interest in the mountain house – the chalet – a small farmhouse used during the seasonal migration when farmers brought their cattle from the valleys in the summer months to graze the mountain slopes. They lived in the chalets for at least the summer months, sometimes sharing them with the cattle during the winter, too, so it was essential that the houses be constructed to be totally weather proof.

The chalet evolved over time. It was, of course, first and foremost, a practical building, with every aspect of its design turned towards making a dwelling that was as durable and comfortable as possible. The ground floor, where livestock would be stabled, would be made of local stone, and outside, against the stone, were stacked layers of firewood – simple storage and also a further layer of insulation. Above, the first floor, where the family would live, was made entirely of timber or with timber cladding over more stone. Local wood would obviously be used, particularly spruce, which has a high tannin content, making the wood darken with exposure over time. At first-floor level a balcony surrounding the whole building was used to dry clothes and store fruit and vegetables, and sometimes a second floor would be added to serve as a hay loft or storage area. The roof, which sloped sometimes quite sharply, was built with wide eaves for further weather

Above *The classic wood and stone chalet sits proudly and practically in its mountain setting, welcoming skiiers after a day on the slopes.*

Opposite *The greatest skill when building or restoring what is to be a country retreat is to use the landscape wisely. No architect could create the dramatic natural spaces of the countryside, and it is important to work with, rather than against what is there. A hillside house sits amongst the ancient terraces, rocks and olive trees, a new part of an old landscape.*

protection, and was tiled with slates, slabs of limestone or thick, carefully weathered pieces of spruce.

Often built somewhere quite close to the chalet would be what was called a *mazot* – a small, sometimes windowless hut, but sometimes a miniature chalet in which valuable items were locked away during the winter. They were originally built as a place where possessions could be safe from the fires that sometimes caught hold of the dry wooden chalets. There are still many *mazots* around the mountains, and many of them have been restored and renovated into small holiday houses.

Some mountain areas are little but rock and dry scrub, and these, too, have their aficionados. On the mountains that fall towards the sea, there are often houses where the occupants can enjoy the relative cool of the higher planes. Retreats built here can be renovated simple dwellings, based on an existing building, or sometimes new structures, designed to reflect the contours and colours of the wider landscape.

This page *Now a perfect mountain retreat, this one-time old barn is graced with a wide wooden terrace from which to savour the pleasures of Mont Blanc. It is roofed with traditional wooden tiles, and the logs stored beneath the eaves add insulation as well as some old-world charm.*

Opposite *A perfect example of sympathetic restoration, it is hard to tell what is old and what is new. The use of traditional materials means that every element works together to produce a warm and comfortable environment.*

A TERRACE IN THE SKY

In this sleepy village in the Valais, which enjoys a breathtaking view over Mont Blanc and Mont Vélan, the lanes are steep and narrow and the silence is deep. This is Commeire, a hamlet of twenty-five souls, where Geneva, only two hours away, seems to be a different world.

Deserted after the war by its farmers, who went in search of an easier life in the valleys, Commeire has been reborn thanks to the dream of Belgian Ludovic Orts, the founder of Montagne Alternative. The adventure began, slightly by accident one day, when out walking, this mountain lover came across this little paradise of age-old barns. That was it – after a lot of thought, Ludovic decided to leave Brussels to buy and restore – one by one – these beautiful buildings, for which he enlisted the help of Benoit Greindl. He christened the project Montagne Alternative.

The first barn that he acquired he restored for himself, christening it Six Blanc for the mountain in front of him. And now, little by little, the old wooden buildings have been brought back to life and transformed into contemporary getaways – for weekends, or longer stays. Obviously it was necessary in such a setting to renovate in a way that respected the surroundings and the local traditions. The façades are kept intact as far as possible, and all the renovations have been made by local workmen who know and respect the environment. Mounted on bases of stone, the five barns now brought back to life have all been restored according to the same principles. The

interior walls of timber, the internal beams – everything has been done to keep as much as possible of the original feeling of the building. Only the roofs have been replaced, and wooden balconies added. Large glass-panelled doors punctuate the outside walls, bringing the majestic panorama into view.

To help them in the design of the interior spaces, and to arrange the rooms, the two friends engaged the architects Devanthéry & Lamunière, who have designed spaces filled with diffused light and soft wood. The decorative element has purposely been kept simple, in order not to detract from the overpowering landscape.

Ludovic has also, where possible, used alternative technologies, such as solar hydraulic heating and roof insulation. Much of the furniture has been made on site, using some of the larch wood recovered during the restoration work. To these were added some old pieces found in Belgium. The result is eco-friendly havens with the air of a chic mountain hotel. A perfect solution!

Above *Wood-clad walls throughout the building, including the kitchen area, give an overall feeling of warmth. This kitchen, as neat as a ship's galley, is designed to make the maximum use of a small space in an efficient and sympathetic way.*

Above right *The large glass-panelled door beyond the dining table is, of course, something that would never have been seen in an old chalet, but what a difference it makes, opening the space and bringing the glory of the mountain landscape into the very room.*

Above *Slatted windows allow soft, diffused light into the room, which is of simple design, with a deep shelf beneath the window that acts as a work surface and also as a storage space where logs can be kept.*

Left *There is a calm feeling to the design and arrangement of these rooms, a sensitive blending of the old and the new, so much so that it is difficult to see quite what has been done where. The sympathetic use of wood, as well as the clever, subtle lighting, all work towards a harmonious whole.*

AN ALPINE JEWEL

All across the Alps new houses are springing up outside traditional villages; advertised as chalets and often presenting a façade of sloping roofs and wooden balconies, inside many of them bear a closer resemblance to a city apartment than an Alpine retreat. So it is refreshing when a traditional **mazot** *is restored and rejuvenated with a light hand – enough to make it a comfortable yet appropriate modern mountain retreat.*

Here, in the picturesque village of Troistorrents in Switzerland, one such traditional mountain hut has been updated for the twenty-first century. The space was originally a shepherd's mountain shelter built in the eighteenth century – charming, but badly situated. To physically move it would be very difficult; to give it a soul would also be difficult, but rewarding. Antique dealer Gerald Lange found the solution by asking his architect, Martin Dauner, to retain the traditional appearance of the hut while bringing the interior up to date, to make it both contemporary and functional. These huts were used not only to store summer harvests during the winter, but

also the village festival costumes. Gerald wanted to rearrange the space, using the height of the structure; Martin suggested using bookshelves in red and grey oak, to complement the solid traditional wooden structure. New windows afford panoramic views of the mountains.

The door opens directly into the kitchen/eating area and on each side of the room there are small bathrooms, all finished in a grey tadelakt, a Moroccan lime plaster. Traditional narrow miller's stairs lead up to the first floor into a living room and bedroom. From the granite-floored terrace the view takes in the Dents du Midi, a majestic background for the half-wild,

Opposite *A mazot, or mountain hut, set in the Alpine meadows. Traditionally used by farmers in the summer when cattle were grazing the lush mountain grass, many of them are now being converted into perfect mountain retreats.*

This page *Simplicity was the key to converting the space in the mountain hut; when space is limited, every extra addition is a distraction. Deep shelves in oak against a rich red background add colour without detracting from the original structure.*

half-natural garden, where there is no trace of exotic imports, just a garden of field flowers, poppies, buttercups and clover.

While the hut itself has been left intact, the base of the building has been rebuilt in concrete, which provides support for the existing building in a way that is both aesthetically compatible and reassuringly practical, and allows the open space that is found beneath all these traditional huts to be retained. Originally designed to ventilate the building, today this space works to bring daylight into the kitchen and eating area. Decoratively, the architect has played with a red palette, adding furniture and accessories from the 1930s. And as for the Swiss art objects that Gerald Lange has collected, they have slipped lightly into place in their new, restored home.

Below *In many ways, the hut appears as it must have been when first built; it is only on second look that you notice the new windows, discreetly installed to add much-needed light to what would once have been virtually daylight free.*

Right *The smallest of kitchen spaces, but all that is needed; anything more elaborate would be out of place in such a compact space, and here everything that is needed is available and to hand.*

A picture of the Alps in summer that Heidi would have recognized, as it was in a hut just like this that she spent her time, in the famous children's book. The exterior has been left in its traditional form, and is all the better for that.

Left One of the bathrooms, finished in a Moroccan lime plaster tadelakt finish, has exactly the right balance of functionality and contemporary style. A well-placed mirror reflects daylight into the room.

Above The base of the structure has been strengthened with concrete, providing support for the original wood-framed building and adding another dimension to the mazot, making it an even more perfect Alpine retreat.

THE TRIUMPH OF THE TERRACES

*Its whiteness sharply silhouetted against the deeply wooded hillside, this finca in Ibiza –
half contemporary, half traditional – is the result of two very different styles
of architecture that work in a surprisingly successful way to emphasize
the pleasures of island living.*

Its owner, Michel, first found the finca, with its traditional tower, in the small ads of a newspaper. Described as 'a baby tortoise squatting on the hillside' and without electricity or water, it immediately appealed – perhaps not so much for its resemblance to a tortoise as for its link to the little stone houses of Provence that cling on rocky terraces to the side of the unwelcoming hills. To others it might have seemed unprepossessing, but Michel was taken with its dilapidated state, and even its diminutive size.

Through a friend, Michel called the Parisian architect Pascal Cheik Djavadi, whose style he saw as open, even Gaudi-esque; he gave him carte blanche, and so, to the existing building,

Below *Like an ancient ziggurat, this restored Ibizan finca marches down the hillside while managing to blend seamlessly into the hillside and surrounding landscape.*

Opposite, clockwise from top left
A geometric cube, part of the new design added to the old by architect Pascal Cheik Djavadi, in tune with the original building but swinging upwards and outwards, extending the overall area.

A perfect pool, inviting and cool, edged with decking made of iroko wood and with a lip that seems to flow into the surrounding hillside vegetation.

A shady area through which the sunlight is filtered, perfect for al fresco life on concrete platforms softened with oversized cushions.

A simple shelter for eating, with rough logs set into a concrete base holding up a palm awning that shelters a table and chairs.

Pascal began to add volume in the form of geometric cubes. It was only then that Michel realized that his little tortoise had become a giant one, with a shell that had swollen all round by 3.5m (11ft), while the tower had gained 7m (22ft) in height. The rigorous architecture, designed to protect the house from the sun, meant that Michel would not be able, as he had dreamed, to use the kitchen and see outside at the same time. These and other such differences of opinion meant that Michel finished the renovation with the help of his partner Kareme.

But in spite of, or perhaps because of, all the artistic and aesthetic differences of opinion, the finished house is today a happy combination of ideas and personalities, with a quirky charm. This is a house where everything revolves around life al fresco – on one side of the outer stairs is a runnel in white cement where water runs down towards a swimming pool edged with iroko boards, with shaded seating areas and a summer eating corner under a palm awning.

Inside is cool and calm, with white painted walls, heavy beams and a kitchen that again combines the past and the present – with an old sink hewn from stone and a central island in polished granite, as modern as can be – and that opens onto a terrace for breakfast. The old adjoining tower is now a guest apartment for lucky friends. All in all, a telling example of the attraction of opposites.

Above *Clean but not clinical with its old sink carved from stone and a new granite work island, this kitchen is functional above all. It's also airy and light due to the low-set windows and high ceiling beams.*

Opposite *The original existing beams become the decoration in this simple, comfortable bedroom, where a fan moves the slow air and a glass door leads out onto a terrace beyond.*

Coastal Escapes

Why do we love to live beside the sea? What is it that pulls us towards it? For some it might stem from childhood memories of carefree bucket-and-spade days on the sand, for others it might be the romance nurtured through books, poems and pictures.

For others still it is just a deep need to spend time in and around the water and its surrounding landscape – the beaches, dunes and downs, the cliffs and creeks, ports and boats. The sea is an ever-changing picture – whether it is the grey-blue Atlantic with waves that can billow and froth, or the soporific seas of the south, the Mediterranean or Adriatic, which on some days barely seem to move, with just the flicker of a ripple on the flat surface of the water. Then there is the air – filled with the scent of salt and seaweed in the north, thyme and rosemary in the south – always a tonic, whether invigorating or relaxing. And the light, the way the sun is diffused by the reflections of the water; in the south it is bright, pure, and sometimes blistering, and in the north it is softer, greyer and often breezy.

Such very different climates require rather different architectural styles – on the one hand a design is called for that will protect from the heat and rays of the sun, while also embracing it; on the other, cooler hand, what is needed is a

Above *Every coastal escape needs a commodious terrace from which to view the terrain and the sea in comfort. This airy example has split-cane blinds that give privacy without blocking the breeze, as well as imparting a soft dappled light over the whole area.*

Opposite, clockwise from top left *Old stone walls, vines, olive trees and hills, with the sea in the far distance, make a winning combination of all the elements that comprise the perfect coastal landscape.*

The slatted sides and roof of this seating area allow air to circulate freely in a constantly changing play of light and shade, while keeping out the burning rays of the sun during the hottest part of the day.

A beach lover's dream: far enough back to provide shade, as well as room for a table where lunch and drinks can be taken in comfort, with comfortable chairs that can be moved around to let you gaze at the endlessly changing sea.

design that can offer not only refuge from too much heat, but also shelter from wilder weather. This accords with the history inherent in traditional seaside architecture. In contrast to that of inland houses, domestic architecture around the coast was always planned with an inbuilt element of protection against the elements – against the unpredictable nature of tides and sometimes even tempests, as well as against extremes of heat and sun. This is one of the reasons that clapboard cladding – a traditional Kentish finish – has been exported all over the world; the layered, overlapping boards, made from a variety of wood from spruce to cedar, encourage rain to drain away fast, thus preserving the exterior of the house from the harsher elements, as well as providing insulation.

Open, flexible living spaces seem to work well in coastal homes; spaces where the cooking and eating blur into one, often coupled with an informal living area, which is quite often equipped with an open fire – welcome more frequently than one might think. Bedrooms are simple and flooring is easy to maintain. These are houses that are designed for easy living, with all that the phrase implies.

There is enough flamboyance, in terms of colour and shape, in any coastal setting so it is not necessary to complicate matters by bringing in competition with the furnishings or the colour schemes. Low key usually works better than high drama. The colours of the shoreline and the sea itself are a good guide: in the sunny south, try colours that are a little warmer, a little brighter; in the cooler north, softer, more subdued hues work well. Take into account that sea air will fade fabrics and paint – not necessarily a bad thing.

Any coastal home should work with the natural features of the terrain rather than against them, and this means working towards the sea. If there is a view everyone will gravitate towards it, so a coastal house must not only have enough windows on the sea-facing side, it should also have doors that open outwards. Ideally, there should be generous porches, terraces and other outside areas that connect directly with the interior and become an extension of the house. This is not the place to have marked definitions between living areas – inside and out should work as one.

Above left and left *Wood and the sea go well – perfectly even – together. As it weathers and bleaches wood looks, if anything, better than when it is new. A pair of painted wooden classical Adirondack chairs looks out over an estuary, and a simple painted wooden door in a wall promises a secret garden within.*

Opposite *Many houses on the coast are high above the sea, and a wooden deck where the view can be enjoyed is a pleasant addition to a seaside garden. Built out on the edge of the rocky land and surrounded by pines, this deck – with its comfortable seating and low tables – is a popular place for sunset drinks.*

ATLANTIC IMAGINATION

The internet is a wonderful thing. This old house, in a hidden corner of the south of Brittany, with its majestic sea views and rich marine landscape, was discovered on the internet by Sophie and Jean, when more conventional searches for a large old villa ready for conversion had failed.

Once the house was bought, a sympathetic designer was required; look no further – the internet yielded up Frédéric Tabary at nearby Nantes, who understood the requirements and parameters for renovating such a house.

On the ground floor, to divide the space sensibly and to open the house onto the sea, Frédéric conceived of one large area – part living room, part kitchen – the whole divided by sliding

Above *Breton houses in the north of France on the Atlantic coast are rugged and well built to withstand the sometimes inclement weather. Coastal gardens in this part of the world must be carefully planted with species that can survive wintry breezes and temperatures.*

Opposite *Sympathetically restored, the kitchen end of this restored old house combines the old and the new. Red metal chairs and the original encaustic tiles add life and colour to the neutral tones of the kitchen furniture.*

glass doors that disappear into the wall. The central cooking island, which is the hub of the kitchen and made from stained and polished wood, is surmounted by a commanding reeded glass hood that hides both the microwave and the ventilation system.

Beyond this sits a large wooden dining table, made in Frédéric Tabary's workshop. The space and its perspective are defined at one end by the imposing stone fireplace, and at the other by the old wooden staircase – which, along with the patterned cement floor tiles, are the only remaining elements of the original house.

The fireplace end of the room has high cupboards that run from ceiling to floor, made practical by the inclusion of a hidden metal ladder installed on a permanent rail so that the higher shelves can be easily reached.

Upstairs, in the master bedroom, Sophie and Jean decided to knock down the partition walls to create a larger space with a central bathroom and views across to the sea. To create a visual division, they used the trunks of weathered trees – found, of course, on the internet – embedded into concrete for stability.

Other bedrooms and bathrooms are equally original – the whole house is a perfect example of a holiday home that is both fun and extremely comfortable.

Opposite *The two parts of the downstairs space – the living and kitchen areas – are divided by metal-and-glass doors that slide unobtrusively into the wall. They define the different areas without separating them. The kitchen table was purpose built to fit the space with precision.*

Above right *Painted wooden open cupboards and shelves run around the living-area walls, making space for objects and books displayed in a pleasing fashion. A discreet metal library ladder on a sliding rail is permanently attached in position.*

Right *Along with the patterned tiles, the curved wooden staircase is original to the house and adds a striking visual balance to the fireplace at the other end of the living area.*

ARCHITECTURAL STYLES

Renovation and renewal

The small, but possibly significant, demographic shift among some of Europe's younger urban population back towards the countryside has meant that conversion, as well as building anew, is in the air. All over Europe – in towns and villages, in fields and woods, on mountain and lakesides, by rivers and oceans – new homes are sprouting up. Some are old houses, cottages and agricultural buildings that are being restored to health and energy, others are completely new structures springing up in the most unlikely of places. And what all of them have in common is a fresh and contemporary outlook on the problems and challenges of creating a holiday home. The solutions and inventive ideas that owners, designers and architects have come up with offer inspiration to all – even to those who prefer to remain ensconced in the middle of the city.

Previous pages *A large old barn has been renovated in such a way that the wonderful original roof beams have not only been restored to their original glory, but also made the central focus of the whole architectural scheme.*

Right *Here, a range of old outbuildings, including a large barn built round a courtyard, has been restored in a sympathetic yet contemporary way; the wide barn doorway has been converted into a glass wall that transforms the entire complex.*

Above left *Barns and other agricultural outbuildings are the ideal candidates for conversion into indoor swimming pool houses.*

Above *On a hillside, this house dating from the early twentieth century looks out over the sea; the rectangular swimming pool reflects the architectural lines of the house.*

Left *Newly built in a wooded area, this family holiday house clad with wooden boarding, and surrounded by wooden decking, seems to blend perfectly and quietly into the bosky surrounding landscape.*

Building styles

When you begin to create – the only possible term – a retreat, how you build and how the final version will appear is dictated very much by how many original elements, if any, you are working with. For some – perhaps the lucky few, depending on your point of view – the site is the only restriction; a brand-new building is going to go up on the spot and all that is necessary is that it works within its context and within the requirements of the new owners. It must also work with, if not be tied to, the vernacular architecture and sit within its natural context. Sounds easier than it is, perhaps, but such an approach, coupled with an open mind, does allow a breadth of imagination that is often not possible when the parameters are more rigid. New ideas can be discussed, new techniques employed and the results are very often as exciting as any other piece of contemporary art.

Left *Uncompromisingly modern, the polished cement wall and doorway of the new building are complemented by the old rough stone wall, as well as the golden gravel of the path.*

Below *Barns and other old, now redundant outbuildings are the perfect candidates for conversion into holiday retreats, providing the maximum amount of space that is flexible and open to alternative architectural and design ideas.*

The next group of builders, the converters and restorers, are those brave people who take an existing house or cottage that has fallen into disrepair – and quite often, pretty substantial disrepair at that, the building having very often quietly crumbled and crumpled over several centuries. These buildings, and what you can do with them, are often subject to severe constraints occasioned by existing untouchable original features. They must be coaxed back into life with sensitive work and a light hand, keeping the features that gave them their charm in the first place, but using contemporary methods and often contemporary materials to bring them smartly into the twenty-first century. The best of them reinvigorate the landscape in which they have stood for so long, combining a nostalgic charm with modern comfort – no freezing cold bathrooms or draughty living rooms in these havens.

And then there are the conversions of buildings that were once for agricultural use – a loose term that covers everything from tiny shepherds' huts to vast barns and equipment stores. With the decline in the West of traditional smallholdings and agriculture, there are many such buildings scattered across the European countryside – some, it has to be said, endowed with more natural charm than others, but all of them a blank canvas on which to make your mark. Depending on how you look at it, these could offer the greatest opportunities of all, or – from another point of view – the greatest of challenges. Regardless of your viewpoint what they do all offer is the chance to construct and create a home that is exactly the way you want it – one that can be as adaptable as your ideas and as practical as your needs. And that must be an advantage beyond price.

Left *In the mountains of Morocco, above Marrakech, a newly built house seems to be both ageless and timeless, using traditional building techniques and materials combined with a contemporary interpretation of the past.*

Agricultural Conversions

Perhaps the most obviously accessible of countryside buildings are those that were once agricultural buildings, but are now no longer used for their original purpose. They are scattered across rural Europe, and are to be found in different states of repair, or disrepair.

Although at first sight, or in an estate agent's window, such buildings can appear rather bleak, not to say daunting, the advantages generally outweigh the problems. Whether they are barns, tractor sheds, stables or dairies, they can be less expensive than conventional houses (which is always a bonus); some – stables and old barns in particular – can be very beautiful, and they usually sit well in the surrounding landscape.

But best of all, perhaps, is the fact that for those with an open mind and a creative bent, farm buildings offer the freedom to bring imaginative and creative plans to fruition and that is worth much, in anyone's book. The internal volume, due to the previous life of the building, will usually be large enough to allow for lateral thinking – indeed, very often only the outer walls need to be retained.

What almost all these buildings lack, of course, is natural light – not surprisingly, never the first concern of the original builders of barns and storehouses. Happily, most barns and machinery stores have wide openings originally designed to accommodate hay wagons, carts and tractors, and are thus

Opposite left *Unusually, this barn has had both entrances, opposite to each other, converted into glass walls, thus changing the building into an open-plan design of the most radical kind. When there is as much exposure as this, every piece of furniture must be chosen – and placed – with care.*

Opposite right *Some of the most successful agricultural conversions are those that literally incorporate the surrounding countryside into the design. Here, an existing tree has been given a commanding and important position in the scheme of things: a veritable living design statement.*

Right *If a building is old enough and beautiful enough then any changes made during restoration should be done with sensitivity. The beautiful stone walls of this old barn have had new windows and doors added in a sensitive and discreet manner.*

tailor-made (almost) to be brought into play as doors and sizeable windows to bring both daylight and the wider landscape inside.

Then there is volume: many of these buildings are tall and often blessed with massive beams and rafters, which have a solid, purposeful beauty. These can not only become the aesthetic focus of the entire space, but also can be used as the basis of mezzanine or gallery floors for bedrooms, bathrooms and private retreats.

Which, of course, leaves the floor space free to be designed to work with any combination of lifestyles and uses. Many use the space in its entirety, and rather than breaking it up into separate rooms, create zones and areas that will flow into each other, each area informing the next – a way of working that is often more in keeping with, and in proportion to, the dimensions of the building.

The materials used are also most successful when they reference the building's original use – even better when they are from the same stock; metal, stone, concrete even, rough wood and plaster. These are not the homes where fancy finishes are to be found.

Decoration too is best when it is welcoming but not precious: rough plastered walls, painted in colours that reflect their surroundings; furniture and furnishings that again are fit for purpose, and in proportion to the surrounding space. They will be inviting, and above all comfortable – where informal relaxation is the aim.

Below *An obvious use for a high-beamed barn is as an indoor swimming pool. This example is designed so that it becomes an integral part of the house beyond, the glass wall bringing the two areas together in dramatic conjunction.*

Opposite *Roof beams in their original untreated or dark-stained state can often appear too dominant in an otherwise cool decorative scheme. Here, the beams have been painted as white as the rest of the room and merge into the vaulted roof above.*

This page *The cooking and eating area is far more than just a kitchen and a table; the furniture and kitchen units work well within the industrial framework, and the painted floor rug is both practical and enjoyable.*

Opposite *Every element of the original, apparently unprepossessing agricultural building has been brought into play to make this the perfect holiday retreat. A corrugated-iron roof over metal supports makes an ideal sheltered eating area.*

INDUSTRIOUS CHARM

It is relatively easy to transform an outwardly pretty building into something that will work for modern holidays; it is perhaps less easy to work such magic on what is outwardly a very unprepossessing building – built strictly for business of a resolutely agricultural nature.

Such was the challenge that decorator Annick Lestrohan set herself – to turn a modern, rather industrial farm building into an informal holiday home; her budget was small, but luckily her ideas were legion.

Well situated among apple orchards and olive groves, this old, very utilitarian building – which may well have been used for farm machinery as well as the storage of crops – had the advantage of very tall iron sliding shutter-doors the length of the building. The only external change that Annick made here was to add, inside them, French windows and doors, half metal, half glass, which matched the existing shutters and were painted, like them, in a red anti-rust paint.

The volume and original structure of the building were ideal for conversion into a casual, relaxed holiday house. The floor throughout was finished with polished cement, and a large fireplace – of iron and concrete and open at both sides – was installed, neatly separating the living area from the kitchen area, which boasts a 'rug' hand-painted by Annick directly onto the cement floor.

Throughout this space, as through the rest of the house, Annick has chosen the simplest, and in many cases the most inexpensive of furniture, which not only fits the limited budget, but also the utilitarian signature of the original building.

Also on this ground level are a pair of simply decorated bedrooms, which open directly into the garden. But Annick had not finished with the sleeping arrangements: because of the immense height of the building she was able to create a spacious children's dormitory, building a mezzanine gallery at one end of the space, above the living area. Up here, the beds are arranged into small groups and separated from each other by the simple but effective device of mosquito nets from IKEA slung over ropes attached to the walls.

Right *A floor of polished cement is compatible with the architecture and perfect for the building's use as a holiday home. The large iron and cement fireplace dominates the centre of the room, separating the different living areas and acting as a natural focus.*

Opposite above *In a clever use of the natural height of the building, a mezzanine gallery has been constructed. It runs along one end of the building, making a children's dormitory where groups of beds are separated by airy curtains made from Ikea mosquito nets.*

Opposite below *On the ground floor, two bedrooms lead directly outside. Within the original metal doors are glass and metal portes-fenêtres that match the originals and are painted in the same industrial red paint.*

Above *The perfect al fresco eating place: directly outside the doors a deep, simple pergola has been erected, with metal posts holding up the wisteria that winds its way around them and spreads out across the top, providing a shady and verdant eating spot.*

It was obvious that a shaded terrace of some description would be a necessity and Annick erected a pergola immediately outside the building, over which a wisteria and a vine now climb, shading a simple dining table of old boards, colour-washed black, which rests on a pair of builder's trestles.

Instead of a conventional swimming pool, Annick designed a piece of water – described as a cross between a farm animals' watering hole and an Andalusian pool. In the form of an 'H' it becomes a smaller pool where children can play connected to a larger, deeper one, and blends well into the surrounding natural landscape.

BARNS AND BEAMS

This conversion is a text-book study in how to convert, in a contemporary and imaginative way, an ancient barn of vast proportions.

Steve is the founder of Buzzispace, a company specializing in the arrangement of office space, and Sas is a designer – the perfect combination to take on the task of transforming the barn into a family home.

When Sas and Steve found the barn four years ago, it had been abandoned for at least ten years and was being utilized as a garage space for old cars. The barn was ancient – dating from the seventeenth century – and the task in hand was to work out a way to make it a modern family home while keeping the unusual and irreplaceable sense of space.

The original brick walls were there and many of the beautiful old structural beams – both the vertical ones and the roof

beams. They wanted the vertical beams to be an integral part of the design, so each piece of wood was cleaned and brushed and then attached securely to the floor with blocks of Belgian stone.

Above left *One side of the swimming pool is planted with grasses and country plants, making it even more part of the landscape. Olive trees and comfortable chairs make the place a restful, relaxing part of the garden.*

Above right *Abutting the barn and perfectly in keeping with the original architecture, the dark waters of the limpid pool, edged*

with simple cobbles and stone, reflect the barn's old stone walls and sloped tiled roof.

Opposite *In an imaginative yet sympathetic design, the original roof beams of the barn dominate the living area, stretching up into the vault of the roof. The vertical beams, anchored in stone, become architectural features, around which the room is arranged.*

This page *The traditional building elements, such as the old beams, are offset by the uncompromisingly contemporary, such as the inset fireplace and the dramatic light, suspended from the roof and centred over the seating in front of the fire.*

Above *High under the roof, the bedrooms are simple but comfortable; this is the principal bedroom, where furniture is kept to a minimum and the colours are deliberately calm – neutral shades balanced by warm, muted colours of the earth.*

Above right *Access to the upper floor and the bedrooms that run down one side of the vast space and round behind the chimney breast is gained by two symmetrical staircases, which lead to a wooden floored walkway demarcated by black metal railings.*

This was not as easy an operation as it sounds – directed by architect Wouter Lucas Andries, each immensely heavy piece was lifted by seven men and then attached to the stone blocks.

The resulting volume, though, free of such minor encumbrances as dividing walls, is impressive – the space is 12.5m (41ft) high and an immense 34m (112ft) long, with 600m² (6500ft²) of living space. Within the huge expanse is a living area centred round a modern fireplace set into a clean-lined chimney breast. An oversized dining table stands between this and the integral kitchen, which runs along one wall and is connected to the rest of the living space by an island counter and worktop.

Intelligent thinking has meant that the space into the vaulted roof has also been allowed to remain free. Two symmetrical staircases – one beside the chimney breast, the other beside the kitchen area – lead up to the galleried first floor, where a walkway with iron railings and wooden floors runs around the space to the bedrooms. Beneath the sloping roof there are the boys' bedrooms (three of them, with a bathroom) while at one end is Sas and Steve's refuge – a bedroom, dressing room, bathroom and study. Up here, as throughout the rest of this cathedral-like space, the colours are muted, soft and natural – chestnut, taupe and old rose, mixed with soft greys and oyster.

LIGHTER THAN WHITE

In the middle of vineyards, ringed round with hills, with Mont Ventoux and the Dentelles de Montmirail behind, an old farm and winery takes on a second life, thanks to the combined talents of a couple très design!

It is the story of an old, abandoned stone building in the middle of nowhere, brought sharply up to date by a young couple – Benjamin, a designer, and Katja, an interior architect and the daughter of an architect.

Katja is Scandinavian and wanted to bring the sense of northern calm found in Scandinavian design into this southern house. Architecturally, they wanted to preserve the simple lines

and the rustic character of the building, and so they retained the openings on the south side – the random small windows and the large ground-floor openings that once led to the animals' quarters and the farm machinery store.

While the exterior is still very much of its time and place, inside a cool wind of modernity and simplicity, certainly Scandinavian-inspired, reigns. Cool pale grey ceramic floor tiles

Opposite *Once abandoned, now restored, this simple and rustic farm building has become a gracious and generous house, its long low lines sitting comfortably among the vines.*

This page *Inside, the look is contemporary in thought, but simple in execution. The overall theme is one of simplicity, exemplified here by the full-length, metal-framed mirror propped, seemingly casually, against a wall.*

run across the ground floor. Divided by the original vaulted doorways, and with a central chimney breast, the living room looks out through arched windows onto the Luberon landscape beyond. There is a seamless transition between this space, the dining area and the cool, modern kitchen. A staircase with a narrow iron guard-rail leads up the bedrooms, which lead off from a gallery. Outside, a shaded terrace leads down to the striking swimming pool – a long raised canal faced in stone, beneath an olive tree.

The approach is uncompromisingly contemporary, but it is neither out of place nor out of style; it works not only because there is a strong design ethic and discipline running through each space, but also because everything from the lighting to the different types of seating and even the decorative touches has been carefully – and cleverly – thought through. In terms of colour, the neutral, even tones and textures are broken with short, sharp bursts of colour, in keeping with the surrounding countryside that combines sun-bleached landscape with sudden splashes of Provençal colour.

Opposite *Grey ceramic tiles run across the ground floor, a visual reference for the interior fittings. The architectural story is one of arches – both the original arched farm doorways and the new arched windows that gaze over the Luberon landscape. The considered, clean lines of the furniture, as well as the complementary decorative accessories and the lighting, make for a calculatedly cool setting in an area where the temperatures can be high during the summer.*

This page *Scandinavian design-think is evident in all the furnishings and decoration in this converted farm and winery. The eating area, which leads from a modern kitchen, is wonderfully cool and simple – an invitation to dine.*

Country Houses

Perhaps the most popular of the routes to go down in terms of the grand makeover is the renovation or restoration of an existing country house – which might be large, but can quite often be pretty small. These are places that are often several hundred years old and that have a place and an identity within the landscape.

Country life was always clearly defined, particularly in mainland Europe, which kept its slower pace and rural traditions for centuries. In a village or a town, everyone had their rightful place, understood by all. There were the local farmers, usually based on their farmsteads outside the village, while within the walls (sometimes literally) would be a mixture of fairly substantial houses for the doctor, mayor, lawyer and priest, as well as smaller dwellings for workers and craftsmen. All was ordered on a well-understood set of unspoken rules, and it is not difficult today to deduce from the style of a country house for whom it might have been originally intended; indeed, much of the pleasure in converting or renovating an old house in the country is in embracing and enjoying this often almost tangible sense of the past.

Above *A solid, reassuring, typical French manor furnished with everything that one might expect: well proportioned with windows at regular intervals, louvred wooden shutters and a garden that relies more on symmetrically arranged paths and lawns than herbaceous borders.*

Opposite *A swimming pool that makes a statement: as clean-lined as the clumps of surrounding cypress, the tidy, shallow stone surround makes this an architectural feature rather than just another pool.*

This page *Typical of northern France, this slightly eccentric, turreted country house is comfortable in its own skin. The whole façade consists of patterns made of brick on brick, both at the windows and on the walls; the theme is even extended to the warm old brick terrace.*

Whether they are the long, low farmhouses and vineyard properties of the south or the sturdy stone houses of the north, built solidly to keep the weather at bay, houses in the countryside welcome rebirth and rejuvenation, and there can be a great sense of achievement in restoring an old house. To successfully renovate an old dwelling is not to reproduce every last door knob and knocker, nor to take out everything that hints of the past, but rather to bring it into the twenty-first century with sensitivity – usually a question of refining and editing, of keeping the best and losing the worst.

A fresh eye on original elements that might at first seem of little value is important. Many an old floor layered with the dirt of years has proved, when cleaned and sealed, to be the linchpin of the entire house. Plastered walls that are uneven in places have much more character than uniform plasterboard, and ceilings that are partially beamed add character to the smallest of rooms.

What is important in an old house is to look at the overall space and to redefine it to suit a contemporary way of living. For some, a clutch of small rooms will not work as well as a larger, more fluid living space, perhaps with a single private area incorporated into the whole. Bedrooms and their attendant bathrooms – or lack of same – will usually need rethinking, as will the access to any garden space and how that might best be used.

Furniture and furnishings, too, need to be chosen with care; very often a mixture of old and new works better than a conscious attempt to recreate a look of the past with nothing but antique furniture, or even to catapult the interior into the present with nothing but modern pieces. As so often in life, a happy compromise is usually best.

Right *The comfort and security of old stone walls: their charm as well as their heat-retaining properties make this a sheltered and warm spot in which to set up a long wooden dining table and chairs.*

THE LURE OF THE LUBERON

Neither the toad-filled pond, nor the broken bits of masonry lying around, dampened the enthusiasm and determination of Laurent and Antoine to buy this seemingly unprepossessing building, even though it was at the far limits of their budget.

Its strength lay in the fact it was in Ménerbes – in their eyes the prettiest village in the Luberon. It was a shepherd's house originally, belonging to the next-door farm, and consisted of a living room, kitchen, scullery and bedroom on the first floor – all very roughly done.

Antoine was a regular visitor to Provence; Laurent, a Breton by birth, did not miss the sea. He preferred the Provençal countryside, which in this area is often buffeted by the Mistral. This last fact meant that an interior courtyard – a barrier against the elements – was the first architectural step they took,

followed by – with the help of local workmen – the remaking and strengthening of all the doors and windows, some in iron and some in wood. The floors were laid with the chalky Ménerbes stone, which has a pleasing crackle effect and needs only an annual protective coating.

Upstairs, on the first floor, walls and partitions have been moved and replaced, woodwork has been painted in soft grey and three bathrooms installed near the bedrooms, ready to receive their guests. Laurent has always had a refined decorative sense and loves to search for the right, unusual pieces for the house. In Paris he goes to the Saint-Ouen flea market nearly every weekend, and in the South he goes, of course, to l'Isle-sur-la-Sorgue. Surrounded by the decorative elements of the house – the antiques, the iron, the painted wood – Laurent worked to simplify the overall look, leaving each piece to stand on its own merits. Old and new are used together. Linen is copiously used to cover sofas and chairs, and with the soft white walls, the overall feeling is one of restful modernity, supported with a few sharp design touches.

Outside, after the space for the swimming pool had been hollowed out and the pool installed, the rest of the garden began to come into focus. The box surrounding the plane trees was trimmed into balls or pyramids, and more lavender was planted between the olive trees and the cypresses, which were

planted in rows – perfectly perfect. But here, again, Laurent wanted to move away from a sophisticated scheme and introduce a simpler, more natural look, in harmony with the hectares of vines surrounding the house.

To live there, year round, would be wonderful – what with the antiques, the garden, the trips to the Sunday market at Coustellet, the Friday market at Lourmarin, and the little grocer's shop at Lumières. Laurent returns from these expeditions with half the butcher's stall, ready to indulge his other passion – la cuisine. The fresh food he finds inspires him with a thousand and one ideas, including quick dishes such as a salad of figs, mozzarella and basil, baked sea bass, sliced dried tomatoes – all delicious. He takes what he can back to Paris to preserve the Provençal dream until the following weekend.

Opposite *The long, low mas of the Luberon convey the charm of Provence with their wooden shutters around doors and windows, and their walls clad with creeper and framed with lavender, topiary and traditional groups of cypress trees.*

Below *The sitting room is a combination of traditional and classic mixed with the contemporary. It is the loose covers, tailored to fit the solid chairs, the simple tables in metal and wood and the neutral colours that make the room new. Easy to recognize, hard to achieve.*

Opposite *Were it not for the contemporary chairs, it would be almost impossible to date this timeless kitchen; an example of clever design, it combines traditional glass-fronted cupboards and a metal-legged table with discreet technology.*

This page *A decorator's dream: a simple antique wooden refectory table contrasting with modern classic – and comfortable – chairs, surmounted with a gloriously extravagant glass chandelier that echoes the collection of antique drinking glasses below.*

LOFT LIFE AU CHATEAU

*Candice de Saint Sauveur sees things on a grand scale: having transformed
the outbuildings of a nineteenth-century chateau in the Perche in Normandy into
comfortable ground-floor rooms for holiday makers, she then went on to transform the
first floor of the chateau itself.*

The style of the holiday apartment Candice created in the chateau owes more to the idea of loft-living than to the country cottage. She began by engaging an architect who specialized in the restoration of old buildings and large spaces. Not, she adds, for the design and decoration of the project, rather to make sure that the essential services and basics – the electricity and heating; the concrete floors, large doors and windows were all correctly installed.

It is a very large space and Candice was anxious to divide it into different living areas, each with its own ambiance, and using oversized furniture and lighting to offset the almost industrial scale. On one side of the space is the living area, where Candice has relieved the starkness of the coloured cement floor and the towering chimney wall – as well as the oversized angled standard lamps – by using comfortable, worn leather club chairs and a leather chesterfield sofa.

Behind the living area is the dining table, 4m (13ft) long, and lit by three huge, cone-sized pendulum lamps. Again the look is softened, here by tall-backed chairs that have been dressed with loose cotton covers in a palette of brick red, taupe and grey – a clever idea she borrowed from a Belgian antique dealer.

The other end of the space is the all-important kitchen – an open space, for practical reasons as well as convivial ones. The central work unit has a surface of anthracite grey tiles, and giant polished grey fruits. A tall, many-shelved cupboard with glass doors holds glass and china.

Leading from the comfortable bedroom, again decorated in tones of grey, is a bathroom that combines the industrial with the witty. Dominated by a large iron armoire, it also boasts a comfortable armchair in deep blue and butter-coloured blinds to soften the light through the large windows. A walk-in shower behind a partition wall adds a final touch of industrial chic.

Left *Restored to life by Candice de Saint Sauveur, who converted the ground floor into holiday rooms, this nineteenth-century chateau in Normandy now takes its rightful place in the landscape, complete with simple formal gardens that rely on a traditional symmetrical plan for their impact.*

Above *On the first floor a loft-in-a-chateau has been created, the large space conquered by the use of over-sized furniture and lighting. The idea was to bring an almost industrial feeling to the space, emphasized by the polished cement floor that is laid throughout.*

Right *Dark bricks, local to the area, are left untreated and in their natural state in a hallway, where they provide a fine foil for a large stone urn filled with plants.*

Far right *Metal is used in abundance throughout this space to create the right industrial loft atmosphere; the perfect material, it is both traditional and yet surprisingly up to date.*

Overleaf *Leading seamlessly through from the sitting area is what could prosaically be called the kitchen. Its laboratory chic, however, makes it something more, as do the deliberately retro furniture and the low-slung industrial lamps.*

New Building

Many of those who want to build a completely new country house, particularly if it is to be a home for holidays and weekends, give as a reason their need for a specific configuration of rooms, as well as a desire to spend as much time outside as possible.

They seek oversized windows and sliding glass doors, terraces that stretch around the perimeter of the whole house and swimming pools – and many of these desirables could never be achieved when converting or renovating an existing building. So they decide to build their own house, and although you might think that to raise a completely new house on a site that is both spacious and beautiful is the easiest of all options, the path is littered with potholes and fraught with possible dangers.

Depending on its physical relationship with other buildings, should the new design reflect the vernacular architecture around it or should it be uncompromisingly different? And, importantly, will it work with the natural landscape in which it is to sit?

Below *Wood to wood: a new house designed not only to fit in with the landscape, but almost to become part of the further wooded landscape. The curves and sweep of the lines of the terraces and the use of stone retaining walls at either end make this a real house of the land.*

Opposite *Building a house from scratch, rather than renovating an existing one, is a wonderful opportunity to make the most of the surrounding landscape, by designing a building in a way that combines open living areas with light, air and space.*

Below *Sweeping living spaces are one of the things that can be achieved when the design is spanking new. The kitchen, always an important part of a country holiday house, here dominates in almost industrial style.*

Below left *Seen from the outside, it is clear that – as was intended – this house as it ages will weather and blend even further into the landscape. The fact that it is built on one level is also helpful.*

Below right *A house consisting of interconnected, almost self-contained spaces embraces the comparatively wild landscape around it in a sympathetic and congenial manner.*

And what about materials? Again, should you use vernacular materials of the district, such as stone from the local quarry, or should you break free from the trammels of tradition and strike out, creating a new vernacular, perhaps – one that will perhaps be emulated in the future?

Such questions are not easy to answer and every situation is unique, but what does appear to be the case is that some of the most successful modern buildings in the countryside today seem to be those that, even if uncompromisingly contemporary in their design, manage to work in some way with the wider landscape, to lie happily within it in an almost organic way. They may be designs that echo the sweep of the land or those that incorporate a particular part of the immediate landscape into the plan, but they are recognizably a small part of a greater whole.

They may also be houses that have taken as inspiration the traditional form of local buildings, from substantial houses to shepherds' huts or farm barns, using the vernacular as a starting point and producing a variation on a theme. Importantly, the scale and proportion of any new building will have been carefully considered in the context of its neighbours, although a mirror image is not necessarily – and not usually – the answer.

The choice of materials is of course crucial when planning a completely new building, for strangely it is often this that first strikes the eye, rather than the architectural design or style. Many designers start with the local tried-and tested-materials – wood, stone, brick – and then combine these with more contemporary finishes, such as metal, concrete and glass. If the new complements or blends with the old then it is likely that the whole will work.

Above *Designed by Seth Stein architects, this house, preponderantly built of Cornish slate with cedar cladding, is situated on a steep woodland slope and is designed to follow and blend in with the rugged, natural contours of the land.*

Above right *The slate retaining wall links the outside to the interior and the double-height glass walls bring the two together. In keeping with the ecological ethos of the place, the floors and joinery are made from salvaged elm.*

Right *The house is two storeys high, and the bedrooms on the upper floor lead off a glass walkway that runs around the upper galleried space. A wall of books adds another element to this house of textures.*

~ Case Study ~

THE HOUSE IN THE WOODS

In the heights around the town of Sète, the architect Jean-Philippe Nuel has created a holiday house as white inside as it is black without. It is an homage to the traditional local huts of the area that were once prolific, but also to the work of the artist Pierre Soulages, who famously works with black as both colour and non-colour; the Soulages Museum is in nearby Rodez.

This was a project that Jean-Philippe Nuel wanted to oversee from start to finish – from the exterior architecture to the right pieces of furniture. He was looking for a design that did not mimic the rural architecture of this part of south-west France, but referenced it instead. He decided, therefore, to build over a

Below *Simple and natural are the watchwords in every aspect of the design of this woodland house. Stone, wood and glass are the central materials, colours are no colours – white inside, black out. The combination is calm and restful.*

Opposite *Referencing the traditional local huts of the area – close to the French town of Sète on the Mediterranean coast – the design is based on structural shapes, each one overlapping a little to give an impression of random choice.*

relatively large piece of land a living complex consisting of several small dwellings, each one self-contained and yet relating both in position and design to the others.

In order to build within the spirit of what had gone before – simple huts in the wood – the architect imagined a group of structural shapes, never perfectly perpendicular, a knowing overlapping of four boxes – the main house and three little houses for guests. The main house would have a generous living area and the three smaller guest houses would each comprise simply a bedroom and a bathroom, all with large glass doors offering a view over the sea, the pines and towards the terrace and pool.

Each house is built of wood on stone piers, with pine-wood cladding stained black; the panelling inside is also of pine, this time stained white. The interior colours are

Above left *The main house acts as a mother ship with satellite guest houses clustered around. Beyond the living area a terrace set with large grey ceramic tiles leads towards a swimming pool and the pine woods beyond.*

Above *Compact and fit for purpose, each guest house is built of wood – pine cladding stained black – and rests on stone piers. The original dry-stone walls around the terrace were restored to their honey-coloured glory.*

chromatic so that nothing jars, and the floors are of polished concrete, except in the principal bedroom. The large terrace is set with large squares of grey ceramic tiles leading to the swimming pool, which is also lined in a tonal grey. Around the terrace the original dry-stone walls of the area have been restored.

These outside spaces were particularly important, because when building what is in one sense a housing complex (albeit on a miniature scale) not only should the main living area and the complementary smaller houses work together as an integral group, but also the surrounding space – in this case the terrace and the dominant old stone walls – should enclose and enfold the buildings, to give them a sense of scale and of place.

Above left *Part of the large living area in the main house: every last detail, from chairs to table to paintings, was chosen by the designer, architect Jean-Philippe Nuel. Pine cladding on the walls is painted white.*

Above *In one of the small guest houses, which each consists of a bedroom and bathroom, black metal-framed windows serve as a refined contrast to the otherwise almost overwhelming whiteness.*

WELL-TEMPERED WOOD

In the Cognac countryside, there is a new, contemporary family house, a house that was conceived by an architect whose heart was once in the city, but who has managed to successfully bring the idea of spacious, sophisticated – almost loft living – into the heart of rural France.

Delphine Bouchet moved to Cognac over ten years ago to start her own architectural practice and raise her young family. Her speciality is houses built around a wooden framework, a circumstance that came about almost by accident when she was asked by a young couple for a house of this type. Despite not having done such a design before, she was immediately enthusiastic, and now all her designs are for houses informed by ecological concerns and about using as many natural materials as possible.

Hardly surprising, then, that when it came to building her own house in the country it was to be as natural and open as possible and clad with wood. The plot that she selected was in the middle of a vineyard; having two young children meant that the house should be simple to run and maintain, and the design she conceived was of a space that was largely open plan, and as receptive to the surrounding landscape as possible. She wanted to use modern materials that were environmentally viable and she wanted natural light everywhere. This last wish has been triumphantly realized – light *is* everywhere, due largely to tall sliding glass doors that lead out onto a wide wooden decked terrace. Immediately inside the front door you are in the large living room, decorated in a monochromatic palette of blacks and dark greys, with notes of red and white here and there to lift the scheme; an unusual colour scheme for a rural house, perhaps, but one that works very well. The kitchen runs down one side, and as well as a chimney corner, behind a half partition there is an office/library area. There is an immediate feeling of air and space thanks to the sliding glass doors, which open onto the wide wooden deck. The master bedroom stays with the monochromatic colour scheme, and only the boys' rooms – orange for one, sky blue for the other – unsettle the status quo.

Opposite *An architect whose particular expertise is in houses built around a wooden framework has created a wood-clad building that is both ecologically sound and in tune with the countryside around it – an area of vines and trees*

Below *The open-plan living area is closely connected with the terrain outside due to the tall sliding glass doors that connect the two. Red – a colour complementary to wood – is used extensively in decorative touches throughout the house.*

Just as the house has been designed for easy maintenance, the furniture, too, has been chosen for comfort and simplicity of style. And at the end of the day, when the weather is good, the sun warms the wide wooden terrace, and the space outside becomes an indispensable extension of the house, where the family eats, works and, of course, plays.

Below *The master bedroom, which opens directly onto the garden, is as monochromatic in colour as the rest of the house, but again lifted with flashes of bright red. Strict adherence to a colour scheme like this unifies a small house.*

Right *Every opportunity has been taken to connect the interior to the exterior of the house, whether through glass doors or, as here, with specially designed small sitting spaces – just large enough for a comfortable deck chair.*

This page *At the end of the wide deck is a slatted pergola area, which juts out and breaks up the wood-clad façade. The pergola is necessary for eating outside in high summer, when shade takes precedence over sun.*

MATERIALS
AND FINISHES

Beautiful bones

There is a beauty in the texture of all building materials and a beauty, also, in the right combination of different textures used together. For most people, the first impression of a building – any building, old or new – is not one of form or design, but one of fabric, of material. The construction may be of stone or brick, wood or even glass, but whichever the building materials employed, it is they that are of prime importance and they that anchor themselves first in the mind. This is partly because building materials have a psychological, as well as an aesthetic and architectural, importance: we endow them with human qualities – friendly or forbidding, gloomy or graceful, approachable or austere. We also associate them with sensory qualities – hard, soft, warm, cold. Much rests on the right choice.

Previous pages *Rough-cast plaster and cement, tinted with earth colours, are popular interior and exterior wall finishes in modern country houses, combining as they do a certain rusticity with a relatively low-cost and easy-to-live-with look.*

Right *A combination of every material and texture here, from the wooden Adirondack-style chairs to the moulded concrete bench and raised planters, the poured cement floor, the three-legged stone table and even the hide rug.*

Left *Traditional building materials have – and always have had – a lot going for them. The style of a house is largely derived from the material or materials used in its construction.*

Opposite *Wood has always been popular for building; it is warm to the touch, malleable and infinitely adaptable. Whether used in an uncompromisingly contemporary vein or in a centuries-old traditional form, it always looks right.*

How construction materials inform character

Naturally – in more senses than one – traditional materials are still widely used for both the building and renovation of country houses, particularly those in rural sites where natural materials seem most appropriate. Such materials are often used to partly recreate the past, but they are just as often combined with new, modern materials to create the present, and even envisage the future. Unsurprisingly, stone, brick and wood are the most popular materials: they represent the rural life around them, they are the most traditional and the most natural, too, in the sense that they are taken directly from the surrounding landscape and earth. But also consistently popular are those materials that are man-made – metal and glass – which have both been used in the building of houses for so long that they, too, can seem part of the natural building process.

The style of a house and the impression it makes on the observer are always dictated by the materials used in its construction, for different materials imply and evoke different sensations. Stone, for example, when used on the façade of a building, suggests durability and long life; wood and brick (and its cousin, terracotta) both project textural warmth, whether used inside or outside; while metal and glass, when used in quantity, bring a certain contemporary feeling. Inside, too, the materials used for construction have an influence that is omnipresent: an unplastered stone wall is a strong statement and requires furniture and furnishings that stand up to its rugged charm, while a wall of wood has an altogether different effect, seeming to demand a soft, simple approach to both the furniture and the colours used in its vicinity.

Although each of these materials is a star in its own right, it is difficult to use any one of them successfully without adding some relief in the form of a contrast in texture, for a single material used on its own is almost always overpowering. The interiors shown here demonstrate many instances of clever sympathetic pairings of both texture and colour.

Finally, and most importantly – and as is seen throughout this book – no matter how fine the renovation, restoration or brand-new design of a building, if the materials used are unsympathetic to their immediate surroundings – other houses and buildings – as well as to the wider, natural landscape, then the result will always be unsatisfactory to all.

Below *Wood is used in abundance here: in the floorboards, the wood-clad walls, the beamed and boarded ceiling, the doors and window frames. And yet the overall impression is light, due in the main to glossy, light-reflecting paint that has been used throughout.*

Opposite *There are no soft textures here – every surface is hard, from the cement floor to the concrete steps and glass-and-metal skylight. Even the chairs and lights are black metal. But for all that, the variety of shape makes the room pleasant and appealing.*

Opposite *A stone terrace always works, particularly when local stone is used.*

Right *Dry-stone walls have a traditional charm of their own. A method of building walls in use since the Stone Age, it works just as well and looks just as good as it did in those prehistoric days.*

Below right *An intricate design of shallow shards of slate combined with larger pieces of stone makes a wall of texture and depth that is a decorative statement in itself and needs no other finish to look quite at home in a living room.*

Stone and Brick

Stone and brick have been used since early man began to venture outside his cave – presumably after noticing for himself the insulating and impermeable qualities of his rocky haven – to build new shelters further afield.

He used stone, but also discovered relatively early on that clay could be baked, by the sun or fire, into hard, tough bricks that he – think the Ancient Egyptians, Greeks and Romans – could use for even more elaborate constructions, as well as for hard-wearing, long-lasting floor surfaces. In many ways, nothing much has changed – both stone and brick are just as popular today, the first choice for many. In all their regional variations, they are used across the world both inside and outside the home.

Walls

Nothing is more redolent of country living, whether old or new, than stone and brick. With its instant patina and wonderfully varied texture and colours, stone is a material with which it is hard to go wrong; its warm glow is both reassuring and comforting, as well as beautiful. One of stone's many pleasures is the range of regional variations to be found, sometimes within a very small geographical area. There are shifts in colour, from the blues and greys that are more often seen in the north of Europe to the creamy, golden-pink palette that we usually associate with the south. And then there is the type of stone, which can range from gleaming thin sheets of seal-grey slate to icy, hard granite or gentler travertine and limestone, both with a warm golden appeal. Brick, too, has always been known for its regional variations. Combining clay and minerals, brick making was originally a local – very local – activity, with the bricks for a building often being made on site. The local clay would be moulded into brick form and left to dry over the summer, then fired in a hand-built kiln. The minerals present in the clay would react with the heat of the firing to give a broad spectrum of colour and texture to the finished bricks, and it is these variations that are so pleasing to the eye. Stone used for walls – and, to a lesser extent, brick – is often rendered or given a light wash, a technique that diffuses the surface roughness and softens the effect. Both inside and out, stone and brick can be used in what can be very serendipitous combinations, with brick used as the facing for doors and windows. Together they can create designs and patterns that, like the materials themselves, are often both traditional and local to a specific area of the countryside.

Right *A simple bedroom with a simple stone wall that is in keeping with the plastered ceiling, the beamed and boarded floor and the traditional iron bed. The stone wall has been given a wash – a protective finish that softens the final look.*

Opposite *Old hand-made bricks are so attractive in their variations – of colour, shape and texture – that it would be a shame to cover them with plaster. In this hall the wall acts as a textural contrast to the metal-framed door and the poured concrete floor.*

This page *The exterior stone wall runs the length of the courtyard into the bedroom – a clever device that emphasizes the connection between inside and out. Given a protective wash, the appearance of the stones has been softened into almost a textural wall covering.*

Floors

Probably the most traditional and popular material for floors – at least in the countryside – is stone. Stone floors have been laid for millennia across Europe, both in simple huts and substantial houses. And with good reason, of course: it was relatively easy to come by, originally relatively inexpensive, and always durable. The variety of stone, its many textures and colours also mean that there is a type and a surface for every requirement. As with walls, the type of stone that is used for floors – from York and Portland to slate to marble and limestone – can vary enormously, not only because of local availability, but also depending on how and where it is to be used. Some types of stone are warmer underfoot than others, to be sure, and it is important to take into account how a particular surface will look among the other elements of the room.

Brick, too, is a very pleasing floor material, particularly when the bricks are of a certain age, or hand-made. Again, as with stone, it is the variation of colour and texture that gives brick floors their charm – that and the pattern in which they are laid. Brick floors are rarely laid in a simple, boring block; they may either be laid in wall-like rows, where ends alternate with sides, or in traditional patterns, such as a simple basket weave or – perhaps most pleasing of all – a more intricate herringbone pattern. Brick floors must usually be sealed, as the surface can raise dust; they can also be colour-stained very effectively. As with decorative patterns for walls, brick and stone can be combined on the floor to create pleasing patterns and designs that also break up the area – sometimes necessary when the floor space is large.

Below left *Concrete, wood and stone all work together in this small and definitely simple bathroom. The addition of any other, more refined surface would look wildly out of place.*

Below right *Flat paver stones are set into the floor in an attractive design, with contrasting white pointing, creating a pattern that is more like a rug than a bare floor. The softened effect works particularly well with the wooden boards in the adjoining room.*

This page *Again, a contrast of textures that works well: a solid, wide-slabbed stone floor acts as a base for pieces of furniture from the 1950s that, with their almost flimsy lines, look even more delicate in this setting.*

Wood

The most flexible and good-tempered of building materials, wood is as popular today – both inside and outside the house – as it has ever been. It is multi-functional. It can be used entirely on its own – as seen in mountain huts and chalets, where every surface, wall, ceiling and floors is made from wood, and where the sensation is one of warmth and cosiness.

Combined with other materials, such as stone or hard-edged industrial materials, it acts as the softer-spoken peace-maker. Wood is intrinsically rustic and is thus admirably suited to use in rural buildings; the timbers most suitable for use are those that are most commonly found in the surrounding area, such as oak, elm, pine, chestnut and beech – exotics such as mahogany and iroko seem out of place. And although wood is the natural material for a traditional approach, or for a work of restoration, its malleable qualities and variety of textures mean that it also provides a natural link to contemporary design. And as an added bonus, natural wood acquires a patina as it ages – it simply gets better and better.

Above left *The pleasures of wood are infinite – its texture, its tones, its many guises. Here, an old beam with a peg through it has been cleaned and left in its original, battered glory.*

Above right *Wood can be painted in a myriad of combinations. Unless it is cleaned and primed with care the colour will eventually become patchy and fade, but for many people that is part of its undeniable charm.*

Opposite *When wood is used for an exterior wall, as in the construction of a mountain chalet, it must be treated in order to stand up to the extremes of weather that abound. As it weathers, it acquires a rugged, attractive patina.*

Walls and Floors

Wooden walls, usually constructed in the form of panels, are one of the earliest methods of decorating a room, as well as protecting it. Prized originally for its insulating properties, wood used thus was warm to the touch as well as to the eye, and was generally kept in good condition by regular waxing. Over time, in larger houses plain wooden panelling gave way to panels that were painted and sometimes gilded and further embellished with carving. Today, although walls are often still panelled for their same insulating, acoustic and decorative qualities, the panelling itself is more often simpler tongue-and-grooved boards – so called as they are cut to fit together tightly, which provides a strong join between the pieces. Boards can be hung vertically or horizontally and can be stained, painted or simply sealed, their final appearance designed to fit in with the general

style and decor of the room. If the panels are not to be painted, it is important to consider how much natural light there will be in any wood-lined or part-lined room, as wood can, and does, absorb light – depending, of course, on the type. Unpanelled wood – simple boards, sanded down – can also be hung, either flat or overlapping, and can look very striking, particularly when stained in a strong colour. Stain permeates the wood in a way that paint does not, and is therefore particularly effective on a rough-hewn board.

Wooden floors are familiar to us all, but sometimes we forget just how pleasing a simple wooden floor can be, whether stained, painted, polished or waxed. Wide boards or narrow; oak, elm or pine: there is a warmth to a wooden floor that is permanently pleasing. The floor is such an important element in the design of a room that it is essential, if

choosing a wooden floor, to ensure that the colour and texture complement rather than fight with any wooden pieces of furniture that might be in place. Painted contrasts with polished, and vice versa; ditto dark wood with light. Different timbers can be used together to give interest to the floor – in the seventeenth century, wooden parquet became fashionable for the rich as an alternative to marble. Constructed of different woods for a contrast in colour, parquet floors were made of oblongs, and are still admired today. Simpler, though, might be to use one timber for the main floor, and another contrasting timber for a border that follows the contours of the room. A painted wooden floor is one of the quickest ways to change the look of a room – there are specialist floor paints, although many people like to use paint designed for exterior woodwork. Thin coats of paint are better than one thick one – the former method means that the coats dry harder and wear more slowly.

Opposite left *Modern mountain chalets are still constructed on the same principles as traditional shepherds' huts. A mixture of woods are used throughout, for ceilings, walls and floors, and they are left lightly sealed, but otherwise untreated.*

Opposite right *New and old wood, in complete contrast to each other: a beam that is more a log than a piece of joinery is set above carefully panelled tongue-and-groove boards that are as smooth as the beam is rough.*

Above left *Painted wood in an interior is always fresh and appealing. Here, everything – furniture and walls – is painted white, making the space both larger and brighter, reflecting and increasing the daylight.*

Above *Wooden strips have been attached to the wall and then given a thin colour wash, to achieve a distressed, aged look. In a clever use of space, wooden storage shelves have been washed in the same colour and affixed across the window.*

This page *Wood is often associated with sailing boats and the sea, and a maritime look is easily achieved by painting walls, doors, ceilings and furniture white. Cleverly, though, the wooden floor has been left in its natural state, and has just been lightly sealed.*

Opposite *As useful a technique inside the home as out, overlapping clapboard wood is a quick and effective way to treat a wall that may not be perfect, or to add interest in a room or space that lacks character.*

Traditionally wood is often associated
with the countryside and the sea, and
a nautical look is easily achieved
by painting walls, doors, ceilings
and furniture white. Cleverly
though, the wooden floor has been
left in its natural state, and has just
been lightly sealed.

This basic household technique
across the home as out, overlapping
clapboard wood is a quick and
effective way to treat a wall that
you set out perfect or to add
integral elements or space that
adds character.

Ceilings

All wood ceilings have a peculiarly soothing quality, perhaps because they keep the room warm and insulated. They also seem particularly appropriate to country dwellings, whether they are made from basic planks, cut to fit, as was always the method used in mountain houses everywhere in Europe, or whether they are more sophisticated, contemporary versions, designed to work in simple modern settings. Modern wooden ceilings are often made from machine tongue-and-grooved timbers – an ideal solution as they have the correct rustic feeling, while being adaptable enough to be installed in different ways: horizontal or vertical, painted or stained. Rural ceilings are also often associated with beams – the instant architectural statement. Stained or kept in an untreated state, beams immediately define a room in a robust and confident manner, and are always pleasing to the eye. The space between them can be plastered, or infilled with traditional materials used in non-traditional ways: cane or bamboo, branches and logs that have been split or left whole, even tree trunks – although obviously only from very small trees.

Opposite top *In contrast to the sophisticated plaster wall colour and the polished stone floor, the ceiling in this smart room is an almost naive design of hemp rope stretched tightly in panels between the beams.*

Opposite below left *A traditional chalet layout where tongue-and-groove walls and the surrounding framework are broken up with a ceiling of plaster and beams – a welcome relief in what could otherwise be relentless wood.*

Opposite below right *Sliced tropical tree trunks used untreated on the ceiling give interesting and unusual texture, with no other decoration required.*

This page *Poles, cut to length, are used in an effective and striking way to make a decorative ceiling design and also emphasize the connection with the terrace and trees beyond.*

Stairs

Stairs in buildings and houses in rural Europe – when there were any – were either in stone or wood. Both are good materials for such a use, but for many, wood is preferable, being lighter and warmer, and often with a character of its own, particularly if it was hand-cut originally. If there is an existing set of wooden stairs in a building to be renovated, they may be in need of repair, and if more than one or two steps need work, the whole staircase can be reclad – an overcoat of sorts. If only partial renovation is required, it is worth thinking about how to make the staircase look its best. It might be just a question of sealing, or sealing and waxing or oiling. If, however, the wood itself is

not good enough, or there are too many new patches, a coat (or two) of paint might be the answer. A painted staircase, particularly if it was originally designed as a practical necessity rather than an architectural eye-stopper, can immediately become an important decorative element in a room. It can be painted in a single colour, or with the risers and treads in two contrasting colours, or – as is sometimes seen in early American houses – painted as though there were a carpet runner, with a wide band of colour running up the centre, and a contrasting colour at either side.

Opposite *Double handrails, relatively shallow risers and wide treads give this design a curving grace as it ascends.*

Above left *An old set of wooden stairs, with a patina and slight unevenness where the treads have been worn down over the years, has a charm and style that could not be replicated by a new design.*

Above right *A contemporary take on a traditional spiral staircase, built around a central wooden column, is more generous in feel and open in design than its classical counterpart. The generous treads and risers make this an easy staircase to ascend and descend.*

Metal
and Glass

Glass is one of the oldest man-made building materials, and many consider that there is no more beautiful architectural medium. Widely known and used in the ancient world, by the seventeenth century glass was commonly used in small windows.

Manufacturing advances were speedy and by the end of the nineteenth century plate glass was common, although it was only in the twentieth century that technological advances meant that the vast sheets of plate glass we now take for granted were perfected. It is now seen as the material most representative of contemporary design.

Not just contemporary design, though; in many a renovation it is the use of glass that has been the triumphant unifier between old and new, connecting disparate buildings or parts of buildings, and adding light to what were once dark buildings – particularly farm buildings, such as storehouses, barns and stables where natural light was at a minimum. Glass can be used for windows and doors, or set into a ceiling or roof to bring light to dark passages and corners.

Opposite *The strength and adaptability of metal make it ideal when looking to make the transition between inside and out appear as seamless as possible. Here, a wall of glass is held in place by the narrowest of metal frames.*

Above left *The addition of a glass roof to an outside passage or dead space beside a house immediately changes the whole concept, not only adding extra cubic space, but also giving a lightness to the entire area.*

Above *A metal frame to a glass window or wall can be constructed in such a way that its dimensions and appearance become part of the overall design, rather than simply a structural necessity, as here, where an old barn has been brought – almost literally and through a window – into the main house.*

Opposite *Metal can often seem much less heavy than wood, as exemplified here, where the original metal doors in what was once a farmyard storage building have been retained, bringing light and air into the renovated building.*

This page *Uncompromisingly contemporary, this internal heavy metal door with mesh-glassed portholes is even stronger against the stone floor and the white-painted rough plaster walls.*

But perhaps the greatest benefit of glass in the countryside is that glass walls, whether they are windows or sliding panels, blur the difference almost magically between inside and outside the house, bringing the landscape closer – sometimes almost into the very room.

Metals – iron, steel, aluminium – are decoratively remarkable. In terms of interior design and decoration, they, like glass, work well with both the old and the new, the rough-hewn and the polished – and with both antiques and contemporary designs, in interiors that are strictly traditional, and those that give more than a nod to the new and the modern. Architecturally, of course metal and glass go together like fish and chips, and metal has long been an intrinsic part of country architecture. The metal smith is still an important person in rural life – traditionally, he beat the iron into sympathetic shapes for airy, light balconies, grilles and stair rails, and, of course, originally, he made window frames, as well as making the weatherproof, indestructible doors and windows for agricultural buildings. These days the smith might be involved in making the whole staircase and possibly some of the furniture – beds, chairs, tables. He probably would not make the window frames – they would be industrially produced – but the principle is the same: metal not only looks very good with glass, but, more importantly, the strength of the metal means that it is the best possible material to act as a frame for the glass, particularly if it is a large sheet, in either a window or panel door.

Stairs

A staircase – any staircase – is one of the most difficult elements to get right in an interior design scheme. As well as its necessary decorative appeal, and the fact that the design must be in correct proportion and scale to the space in which it sits, the stairs must be fit for purpose, allowing easy ascent and and safe descent. This means that there are always many technical and practical problems that must be overcome. Today, in modern schemes both in the city and the country, metal is often the material of choice.

In practical terms, a staircase of metal is hard-wearing, long-lasting and needs relatively little maintenance. In aesthetic terms – just as important – the major advantage of metal is that it is so adaptable and can be designed and made in almost any form desired, with banisters and hand rails that can be slender or solid, and risers and treads that can be chunky and heavy or elegant and airy. Metal can be wrought or turned into the most ethereal and narrow of spirals that wind around a central post. Due to its strength, metal is a particularly successful material when employed in a design for 'floating' stairs, which seem to stand almost without support, with just treads and no risers to be seen. Metal combines happily with both wood and glass, another characteristic that suits it well to contemporary living. The juxtaposition of two such different textures can be both appealing and dramatic.

Opposite *When a staircase is needed that will make the most of a light-filled space, metal is the only material that will work. Its strength means that the design of both stairs and rails can be light, almost airy, in execution.*

Right *Metal can be wrought and manipulated into any shape or design. This staircase is a combination of the straight and the curved, and works admirably in a narrow space that leads up to a library gallery.*

This page *Smoother than smooth and twice as cool, this polished cement floor is both stylish, contemporary and immensely practical. Flowing across the whole floor from room to room, it unifies the separate spaces with ease.*

Opposite *Instead of wooden boards, rough-cast concrete planks are used like clapboard for a bathroom wall; in keeping with the workman-like setting, the wooden towel ladder and polished concrete steps add to the pleasant rough-hewn atmosphere.*

Plaster and Concrete

Like so many seemingly modern materials, concrete – albeit in a slightly different form or recipe – was in fact used extensively during the Roman Empire, with many edifices, such as the Colosseum, still standing. Roman concrete was an extremely strong construction material, not unlike modern concrete in composition, although usually faced with brick or some other finish, but the technology was lost after the fall of the Roman Empire and reintroduced only towards the end of the eighteenth century.

For years concrete was always associated with either industrial or urban architecture, but actually it is one of the most creative of materials in use today, as well as one of the most adaptable. It works well in many different guises in the architecture and design of country homes, and although a relatively new material in this context, it has swiftly become widely used. One of the reasons for its new popularity is its adaptability and versatility. Concrete is also tough and virtually indestructible, making it well suited to a space that might not be lived in all year round. Whether it is used in its brutal, raw state or poured, polished or stained, it can work in every room. For a long time, neutral tones were the only finish to be seen – a hangover from concrete's industrial past – but stronger colours are now finding favour. Rough-cast concrete planks are good on walls – the concrete is poured into plank moulds, or impressed with wooden planks, and then turned out and attached to the wall.

As well as being used for floors and walls, concrete is now often cast or moulded into tables and benches, wall seats and worktops – permanent and solid, pieces like this are sometimes coloured with pigment and polished to a high gloss. Fine polished concrete resembles polished stone and has a tactile, sensuous appeal, which makes it as useful for outdoor furniture as for inside the house.

Like concrete, different forms and mixtures of plaster have been used to decorate the exteriors and interiors of buildings for many thousands of years; it is a material so old

Right *The available range and breadth of colours used to stain concrete are vast, ranging from pastel shades to rich, sometimes bright, earth colours. Here, the chimney breast has been stained in a dramatic deep charcoal grey – an appropriate colour for the setting – and is complemented by neutral colours and textures.*

and yet it can look so new – even when the finish is a traditional one, such as the extant painted plaster walls of Pompeii. Outside plaster – render – is a mixture of plaster and cement, popular throughout Europe as a finish to waterproof and protect the external walls. Different areas have very different colour ranges (usually derived originally from the local earth tones) and most buildings look best when finished in a colour that complements the local palette.

Plaster used inside the house is one of the most joyous of finishes, both on the walls and on the floor. It is warm to the touch and intensely tactile, both in its natural state and particularly when it is tinted with pigment and then polished, which can be done either in its natural state or after tinting. But not every plaster surface needs to be tinted and polished: in a renovated old farm building, such as a barn or stable, a rough plaster finish on the walls – where the plaster is applied with a trowel and then left to dry as it is – is often much better looking and more suitable than the ultra-smooth, glossy look of perfection.

Opposite top left *This mountain retreat blends tradition with contemporary sophistication. Although designed in classical mode, this fireplace substitutes a wooden surround for a concrete one, intended to reference the stained boards above.*

Opposite top right *A concrete and cement cocoon, where walls and floor are in tinted and highly polished cement, and the dramatic open staircase is of pressed concrete. The combination of texture and finish is akin to a sculptural installation.*

Opposite below left *Softened with copious indoor greenery, the concrete table and polished cement floor of this garden room make a pleasing and practical picture.*

Right *A coats-and-hats bench and general changing area needs to be efficient and easy to keep clean and tidy. A polished cement floor, coupled with white plaster walls, is a cool background for the solid concrete benches.*

~ Case Study ~

THE HOUSE OF OCHRE

Romain Michel-Ménière is a furniture designer who has turned his attention to interiors, for which he is now internationally well known. He was anxious to return to his roots and build himself a house in Morocco, choosing a site outside Marrakech with a view that stretches away as far as the eye can see, towards the Atlas Mountains.

Michel-Ménière's dream was to have a house on one level, with a garden that was natural and at ease in the surrounding landscape. Although totally contemporary in style, it has an air of traditional Berber building, a feeling of the Medina and the riads. The design is based on the idea of a traditional farmhouse interpreted through contemporary architecture. In this he was influenced by the Belgian architect Olivier Moureau who, in turn, was influenced by the linear architecture of the great Luis Barragán, whose interplay between light and dark, planes and surfaces, created some of the most original houses of the twentieth century. On entering the building, the high walls that divide the space seem to echo the alleys of the Medina; the

shadows cast by them are cut through by the staircase of slatted walnut that crosses the house from side to side and leads to a large terrace, which is divided into two zones – day and night. Inside, the sitting room is also divided from the dining room by a large central open fireplace, echoing the plan of the terrace.

Michel-Ménière has used traditional building techniques and materials, combining them with the modern and the unusual. Within the house, and outside it, he plays with light and shade, with shadow and sunlight. He has brilliantly used traditional materials and techniques, such as compressed clay bricks made from a mixture of earth and straw, palm and eucalyptus trunks for the ceilings, which create a wonderful counterpoint of the

Opposite *Part ancient Berber, part up-to-the-minute contemporary, this house outside Marrakech in Morocco is finished in traditional materials and looks as though it might be part of the Medina.*

This page *Decorated in the warm colours of the earth, the interior space consists of a sitting room and a dining room divided by a large central open fireplace, which in itself is a strong – and practical – design statement.*

rough and the smooth, and a traditional mixture of cement and lime, washed with black-olive soap, for the floors. Old studded farmhouse doors were bought from local antique dealers, with other doors then created in the same spirit.

Throughout the house he has combined old and new, Oriental and European, in what can truly be called an eclectic mix; here, his unbridled imagination runs loose. And why not? As he himself says, 'Rather than invent a Moroccan fantasy inspired by the past, I opted for a mixture of styles. Perhaps one could call it James Bond *chez* the Berbers!'

Opposite *The dining side of the open dividing fireplace leads directly onto the large terrace, which runs across the width of the house. Colour notes are picked up from the seating area such as the rug, which echoes but does not imitate.*

Above *An unusual and effective window frame between the bathroom and the bedroom is edged in cut palm trunks. An old door that echoes the spirit of the design of the house leads into the bedroom.*

Right *This kitchen achieves what is so difficult: to design a room that seems as if it has been there forever, but which is completely up to date. Reflective surfaces add to the impression of longevity.*

COUNTRY
LIVING

Simple pleasures

Happily for all of us, the countryside, despite all the inroads made on its identity, still has a distinct personality of its own – it still functions in its own right as a separate entity, rather than as a sad imitation of the city. Not only is the pace of life very different, but also the pleasures – easier, gentler, warmer even. Such pleasures centre on the home and its surroundings and include the joy of food, well cooked and heartily eaten; of fresh air and of countryside pastimes and pursuits. The life that is led in the houses in this book is the most important thing about them, and every element within them has been chosen and created to bring quiet pleasure to all.

Previous pages *Summing up the visual pleasures of rural living, whether it is in a manor house or a shepherd's hut, is the beauty of a rough-plastered wall, highlighted by old beams that have simply been cleaned and sealed.*

Right *Country living? Yes – resoundingly so but simple modern, rather sophisticated country living. Every design element has been thought through, including the landscape features.*

Establishing a style

The interior of a country house – whether it is a large, imposing edifice that commands its immediate surroundings, or a small converted hut or barn – will always have certain common elements. Natural materials will take precedence over more man-made artefacts. The rooms will be arranged to be flexible, to easily accommodate the few or the many. The seating will also be flexible, and, too, it will always be comfortable – sometimes old, sometimes new, but always chosen for relaxation. The arrangements for cooking and eating will play a large part within the overall interior scheme – and often the exterior scheme as well – and there may be several different choices of places to eat and drink. And most importantly, the interior will always be designed and arranged to relate to the outside world – living things, the landscape, the changing light, the colours and shapes of the countryside.

If there is a lightness of being that is associated with the countryside, then there is also, in the best country houses, a lightness of being within the way a house is dressed and designed. This does not mean that there is any one particular style that works better than any other, it is just that there are certain decorative avenues that are best unexplored. Successful modern country houses, for example, do not groan beneath the weight of heavy, dark-hued, interlined curtains. If there are any, curtains are light and at one with the windows they do not hide. Neither do these houses drown under acres of close-fitted carpets – flooring should look good, of course, but it must also be hard-working, of natural origin and ready to shoulder the daily perils of everyday indoor-outdoor living, in all weathers, without strain or complaint. Furnishing fabrics should be light, in texture and in tone; the colours that work best are usually within a sophisticated palette of

This page *An informed and confident style, here – traditional design, but with a distinct contemporary twist. The style signature is simple, pared down, with little or no extra ornament or embellishment, but everything geared towards comfort.*

Above *A traditional eating space, but more than that, a classical dining arrangement that could work within any style. A wide table covered with a check tablecloth, and surrounded by white-painted wooden chairs, is timeless in their appeal and charm.*

Above right *In a restored farmhouse stripped to its simplest form, with white walls and natural beams, an old, rustic trestle table takes centre stage as the dining table of choice. Waxed and polished, edged with simple wooden benches, it needs no other adornment.*

Opposite *Wooden garden rocking chairs, based on the traditional Adirondack design, are ready for use in this half-way room between the house and garden, shielded from the excesses of weather of whatever description.*

neutrals – not boring beige, but a wider range that runs from cinder and pearl grey to ivory and clotted cream.

Establishing a style also means establishing a way of domestic life that is designed to draw on the surrounding countryside, to make it accessible and part of everyday living. Modern country is simple, in the purest sense of being no fuss and not too many extras. This sort of style means keeping the decorative touches light and modest: too much pattern – indeed, too many shapes – can be hard to swallow, even indigestible. Excess is not allowed, neither are unnecessary frills and furbelows, although some carefully chosen ornament is good, as is the odd witty touch. Above all, comfort should be paramount – although that is not to say that a certain elegance need not be part of the mix.

LOG LIVING

In the middle of the Champagne countryside, a traditional eighteenth-century stone building, once a creamery and shown as such on maps of the period, has been reclaimed and restored by its young owner into a light-filled, contemporary house.

S et within fields surrounded by deer-filled forests, this building has the countryside everywhere around it, and it has been incorporated into the architecture and design of the house, with its stone walls, hand-made roof tiles and – inside – a predominance of unpolished wood, oak beams, rough-plastered walls and simple, solid furniture.

Its owner, Georges, aged twenty-nine when he bought the building – a relatively young age to consider such a large building project – had been looking for a place to which he could escape from Paris, 100km (62 miles) away. He found the creamery, then a ruin, in the Champenois countryside where he had spent some of his childhood. 'It was my dream house,' he says, but a dream he knew he could not realize without the help of his mother, an architect, who agreed to run the project on a day-to-day basis.

Opposite top and bottom *This creamery is a beautiful building of old stone and mellowed, hand-made tiles that replaced the original, ruined ones. Unloved for many years, it has been carefully restored, both inside and out, to produce a building that is now a loved country home.*

Left *Natural elements abound within this old creamery. Every room, every area, has been carefully considered – such as the dining space with its long table standing on sturdy block legs, and stools cut to match.*

The first months of heavy construction work were hard – the foundations needed shoring up and the walls strengthening in order to stabilize the building, particularly when the large windows and doors were installed, which were necessary to bring light into the formerly dark building. And then there were the roof tiles: Georges's mother had ordered 15,000 hand-made roof tiles, in five different colours and three different sizes. Under the sometimes impatient gaze of the waiting team of roof tilers, she mixed together shapes and colours by hand, so that the finished roof would have a wonderfully varied and natural effect.

Meanwhile Georges, from his office in Paris, was sending detailed notes, rough sketches and drawings on a daily basis, as well as the collected ideas and suggestions of his friends, all of them grouped into themes – bathroom, kitchen, lighting, ironwork – and so on. It was, as he says, 'a mad time for the people working on the house!'

But the end result – five years on – has definitely been worth it all. The old farm building is now a place of oversized, well-lit living spaces, with natural materials used in a confident and pleasing way, from the floors of polished cement to the rough-plastered walls and undressed wood. It is a clever combination of unvarnished rusticity and sophisticated comfort – epitomized by the installation of under-floor central heating. No wonder that Georges's new dream is to reverse his current living/working plan, and live in this rustic heaven all week, escaping to Paris for the weekends!

Opposite *The kitchen fits completely into the mixture of part city, part country, with its simple worktops and curtains instead of cupboard doors, on a shining floor of polished cement. The lights are a witty take on the raw wood theme.*

This page *Undressed wood again, but also comfortable chairs and a satisfying supply of wood for the winter fires. The austerity of the polished cement floor is ameliorated by the fact that there is under-floor central heating throughout the space.*

CORSICAN POLISH

*In a truly personal burst of colour, a house that is half African farm,
half loft-chic, built in Balagne in the Mediterranean island of Corsica,
plays with matter, volume and light.*

So totally convincing is the innate sense of architecture, design and decoration displayed by the designer of this almost organic house that it seems to rise from the earth. Marianne Sidler explains it thus: 'We had lived for many years in Africa and Asia, moving twenty-one times, so I have restored and renovated many houses and apartments. So when we found this magnificent corner of land on Corsica, I wanted to design and build a house – our house, because it was always going to be about us – and I have put into it all my ideas and all my passion.'

The idea was that the house would comprise a principal living space with a large outdoor living area and an annexe for friends.

She dreamed of a loft-like space – large (which it is – 17m /56ft long) where she could cook, eat, work and entertain. She wanted it to be several different zones, punctuated by two bedrooms. Above the kitchen area a long glass roof with slanted metal bars brings in the morning light, and on the ground floor bulky, low partition walls, which look as though they were made from African mud, delineate the different areas. The idea was to section off, but not completely shut off, the spaces, for Marianne wanted light to flow through every part of the house. The floor is of poured, polished cement, which accentuates the spaces and also reflects the light.

Opposite left *In front of this African-inspired Corsican house sits a piece of water that looks as much like a village watering place as a swimming pool. It is set on a grass terrace overlooking the surrounding hills.*

Opposite right *The exterior of this new house looks much like an old house – and an old house in Africa at that. The ethnic look has been enhanced by the application of a plaster coating that has the look of sun-baked earth.*

This page *A long glass roof above a corridor at one side of the house is unexpected and brings surprising shafts of light into different areas of the large living space.*

This page *The long living space has two bedrooms leading off it. A polished cement floor sets off a telling mixture of the old and the new – such as a romantic glass chandelier and an antique armchair, coupled with pieces of African art.*

Marianne has also used wood liberally, with shutters in chestnut and tables in oak. The colours reflect the natural essence of the scheme, including soft half-tones that might be of the desert or the kasbah, cool and yet contemporary.

Metal-framed glass doors lead into the garden beyond, where a rectangular pool sits on a grassed terrace looking out over the hills and sea. The façade itself was clad with a sponged coating that takes on the appearance of the baked earth so ubiquitous in the countries Marianne loves.

Above *Comfort is at the fore of this part of the living area, with spacious sofas and deep armchairs surrounding the open fire. Large metal-framed glass doors on all sides mean that the delights of the garden landscape are never far away.*

Opposite *Unusually, in the interior space Marianne Sidler has added bulky internal partition walls that look as though they were made from African mud, and which break up the living area in a sympathetic and original way.*

TECHNO HEAVEN

**On the magical island of Ibiza has risen a modern – very modern – house that
in many ways seems like a dream, a game between nature and architecture,
built on a hill that is far from the bustle of Ibizan holiday life.**

Three pine trees and two palms push up through the roof of this futuristic house, seeming almost to relish finding the blue sky above. The house, built by the Spanish architectural practice Andrés Jaque, was designed to incorporate these living trees, which soar through part of the interior, giving the whole space the feeling of a tree house – although a tree house on a particularly grand and luxurious scale. The whole house seems to embody the free spirit of Ibiza, designed as it is to work with

the natural contours of the site, and specially calculated to minimize harm to the flora and fauna, such as the trees and shrubs that grow around it. It has been built on what might conventionally be seen as inhospitable sloping land, but the design is based on a series of cascading terraces supported by stilts – in reality, concrete piles. The social heart of the house is a large terrace that runs towards a beautiful pool, large and rippling, like a secret lagoon of still water.

The main house is supported on a concrete structure, while the elevated terraces are supported within a metal frame. In the main house, which consists of a large kitchen and living room and two bedrooms, all the rooms are open to the landscape, which, in this instance, is the bay of Cala Vadalla. Leading from this central point, two walkways – bridges almost – lead to self-contained cabins, equally tree house-like. The house itself is called Never-Never Land, while the sheet metal used inside and the decorative interior colours – the blues, the greens, the stabs of contrasting fluorescent colour – all combine to make this a playground in the sky. One cannot help thinking that Peter Pan and the Lost Boys might have felt very much at home here.

Opposite *Like a futuristic craft, this modern Ibizan house on a sloping hill has, instead of the traditional terraces, been built on a series of concrete piles that make up the different levels and that cling to the side of the hill like stilts.*

Below *Inside the cooking and eating area, the design has been so arranged to allow three of the trees that were in situ when the site was found to grow – dramatically – through the centre of the room.*

Above *Open to the landscape as these rooms are, colour is very important. The clear blues and greens, coupled with nature's own palette, add to the light-filled reflective feeling that is everywhere here.*

Far left *When a house is set high in the hills among the treetops, what could be better than to have an almost-outside shower? Metal framed like the rest of the house, it makes the most of the lush green views all around.*

Left *Tinged with the reflections of the landscape, this rectangular pool sits in a large terrace, again built so that it appears less a man-made structure and more a hidden pool floating among the trees.*

This page *A self-contained bed cabin, reached by a bridge-like walkway from the main building, is compact and efficient, and with its porthole window seems more like a child's tree house than a conventional room.*

Living Spaces

A living room today is perhaps – along with the kitchen – the most important room in a house. And that demand can be hard to live up to, for such a room must perform so many roles and be so many things to so many people – something that is perhaps even truer in the country than it is in the city.

Once, there were several different small rooms and spaces, each with different roles – possibly a library, a sitting room for domestic pleasures, as well as a larger parlour, salon or drawing room where friends and family could be entertained. Over the years, though, as life has changed and become more informal, the idea of having one large living space, rather than several small ones, has grown in popularity, and now, particularly in houses that are holiday orientated, very often the entire ground floor is a multi-functional living space. So flexibility is essential; an ability to mix function with form, and informality with purpose. As is always the case, understated is better than overstated, and less is invariably more.

Left *A living area that combines all that is needed in a contemporary country house; first of all, comfort – enough well-cushioned sofas for easy relaxation – and second, quick and easy access to the garden delights beyond the room.*

Accomplishing comfort

A great deal of planning and thought goes into the perfect living space, and however informal the finished look, there will be nothing haphazard at all about the arrangement of the room. In modern country houses the various living spaces all share common themes and considerations: they are first and foremost designed for ease of living, flexibility and comfort – chairs and sofas that you want to sit down on and that can be moved at will; long, low tables where books and magazines can be piled and glasses parked. There is very often a fireplace, which becomes the warm centre of the space, and there is always a wide spectrum of lighting: ambient lighting, of course, but also table and floor lamps that can be positioned wherever they are needed. Flooring is always cool – stone, concrete, wood – and any rugs or other floor coverings are purposefully simple in type and light in weight. As in any room on the ground floor, the relationship with what is outside the room is all-important, and if there are to be curtains at the *portes-fenêtres*, they will be lightweight in texture and in style, so as not to obscure easy access and egress. Any colours employed will deliberately be kept within the neutral spectrum to act as a background for living rather than intrude upon it.

Opposite *Not every country retreat is warm all year round – indeed, some are built particularly for wintry weather. For these escapes, a den-like atmosphere is the key; draught-proof windows with well-built shutters or curtains and warm rugs underfoot.*

Above *The effectiveness of wood as the traditional, perfect insulator as well as the bringer of inner warmth and comfort, is well illustrated here; comfortable chairs and a good fire complete the pleasant picture.*

Opposite *A good example of how a large space can be divided and used as an all-purpose living area: at one end, beneath a low-beamed ceiling, is the cooking and dining area; the rest of the room is given over to comfortable chairs and low tables.*

This page *Simple in concept, but containing everything necessary: solid, old shutters on the wall, hard-wearing leather sofas, a sturdy table and chunky stools make this a room that can be used and enjoyed without fear of damaging anything.*

One-space living

As has already been discussed, the concept of open-plan living might have been invented for holiday homes in the countryside. The idea of a plethora of small – or even large – rooms seems more and more anachronistic; even those who live in town houses or apartments that cannot easily be altered have tended over the last few years to combine the functions of different rooms. And how much more appropriate in the countryside, where different age groups with different interests may all come together under the same roof? Luckily, many country places lend themselves well to this sort of living. Perhaps they have been adapted from an old house with small rooms that devolved into one or two larger spaces; perhaps they were agricultural buildings where the only divisions were between barn and stable; or perhaps they were even newly built – that happy state of affairs where dreams and plans can be executed in full. Open-plan living should be designed to be particular to the inhabitants of the moment; the only general guidance that might be followed is that it is important to work out in advance exactly what a certain space will be used for, and to allow for enough seating and storage to realize the plan.

Below *A cool room, with neutral colours to the fore and a contemporary design for the fire, plus a floor of wide wooden boards and metal-framed, sliding doors that allow the garden to become the main focal point of the room.*

Opposite above *Angled glass diffuses cool daylight across the whole living area. Colours and materials are deliberately kept calm and peaceful so that the room becomes a haven from the heat of the sun outside.*

Opposite below *Although neutral tones are often favoured in contemporary country retreats, it can be a good idea to add short, sharp bursts of slightly off colours to the mix – here, acid-yellow cushions provide the contrast.*

This page *A room designed to be informal at heart and yet arranged so that everything that one might need is close to hand. Deep open shelves either side of the wide chimney breast with room for everything are always a good solution to both storage and decoration conundrums.*

Opposite *A good example of flexible forms, this living area has a multitude of small pieces of furniture grouped around the elongated fireplace that can be employed at will: enough seating with two sofas, small circular tables that can be moved where they are needed and lightweight rustic stools for extra seating when required.*

Fireplaces

The fireplace, or hearth, has always been the heart of the home; in earlier times the fire was the source of both food and warmth. Later, the fireplace and chimney breast together became valued as a status symbol – the larger the chimney piece, and the more ornate and embellished it was, the more important the house owner. And now, after surviving various vicissitudes of fashion, the appeal of an open fire is stronger than ever – particularly in the country, where not only is it a focus and a centrepiece of many a room, but where fuel, in the form of wood, is often readily available and there for the taking. The trend in fireplace design is, at the moment, towards simplicity, in keeping with the rest of the interior design, although simplicity does not necessarily equal small; many contemporary designs make much of the hearth itself, and the wood-burning stove is also enjoying a revival.

Cooking and Eating

Throughout the European countryside, the arts and acts of cooking and eating – particularly when the house is a haven and a holiday home – are possibly the most important activities that take place on a daily basis.

There is, after all, the time for leisured food discussions – what type, when, how much, for how many? Often the local markets are the venues of choice for the next important step – the consideration and deliberation, the viewing, choosing and then, finally, the purchase. And later, at home, the most vital part of the process – the preparation, the cooking and, at last, the eating. No wonder the areas set aside for such weighty activities are so carefully considered and such cause for deliberation. Should the kitchen be large or small? Modern or traditional? Where in an open-plan room should the kitchen be situated? And the dining table? Should it be part of the kitchen? In a separate room? Or indeed should there be different eating spots, both inside the house and out? Many questions, with luckily just as many answers.

Right *A kitchen created for the enjoyment of food – in all its incarnations. Distressed painted wood sets the tone: everything is designed for easy work and easy eating, from the open shelving to the central island and the comfortable wooden table.*

This page *Contemporary in feel, yet very comfortable to work in. An efficient, carefully designed central work island, which includes a double sink and multi-hob, is buffered by two pretty, basic stools – ideal for a cup of coffee or to read over a recipe.*

Opposite *A striking contrast between the outer dry-stone walls and wooden door and the supremely contemporary metal-finished kitchen within. A work machine, everything here has been carefully planned for maximum efficiency.*

Cooking and dining in the same space

Cooking and eating in the countryside should be a relaxing pastime, and for many households, the easiest way of ensuring this is to unite the two activities in one area – a space that will be designed to combine a measurable degree of efficiency with an appreciable degree of comfort. It is an agreeable conundrum, and many modern country dwellers solve it by creating a working area that is often frighteningly fit for purpose, coupled with a more relaxed neighbouring eating area that includes a table big enough to use for preparation, as well as to accommodate as many or as few diners as the occasion demands.

The concept of the fitted kitchen is one that has not always found favour in traditional country homes, which have often been better suited to a more informal arrangement. But in today's country kitchen there is a place for contemporary fitted design – particularly when combined with a more traditional eating space. Many of the most successful combinations in this genre rely on the choice of strongly contrasting materials – austere, almost industrial-looking work surfaces and cabinets, coupled with deliberately traditional, often antique, dining tables and chairs.

Right *A kitchen that doubles as a dining room – or vice versa for that matter – must tread the fine line between comfort and practicality. Here a wide, solid table that is as comfortable to work at as it is to eat at provides the central, unifying focus.*

Compact solutions

Every home – particularly, perhaps, those that are small, such as cabins, cottages and converted huts – needs some sort of eating space and, by and large, some sort of table at which to eat. Sometimes, simply a smaller version of a conventional table might do the trick, but often it is a moment for lateral thinking. In the mountain cabin on these pages, the table cleverly slides into a custom-made space beneath a window when not in use. In a kitchen/eating space, a sliding table could pull out like a drawer from an island worktop unit. Unused corners can be brought into play using bench seats – always a good small space solution – built into each side of the corner wall. There are small square tables with half-moon flaps that extend into a larger round table, and rectangular tables with integral extending leaves. There are circular tables that, when in not in use, can be flipped so that the surface is upright against the wall. Perhaps easiest of all, there are small square tables that can be bought in multiples of two or three and stored around the living space, to be used singly or together as occasion demands.

Left *In the mountains, meals are often taken inside, and space is often at a premium. Good planning and design are essential, as are clever storage and use of space. Splashes of colour in cushions make the area appear larger.*

Opposite *The clever design feature here – a table that slides away when not needed – makes the most of this chalet's limited space. Lightweight metal-mesh chairs not only take up less room than traditional wooden ones, but also seem to disappear into the space.*

Above *A modern, made-for-purpose working kitchen – simple and spare in its lines, with every unnecessary item safely behind cupboard doors – is balanced by the warm antique table, as well as the whimsical: a flying fish that dives from the ceiling.*

Opposite *Colour and convenience meld in this country kitchen. The working area flows down a level to become the dining table in an easy and charming way that makes the best use of what might otherwise be too small a space.*

Making country contemporary

The modern country kitchen is no longer a place of distressed or painted pine with bunches of dried flowers hanging from the ceiling and copper pots gleaming on the walls. Not that there is anything wrong with any of the above, it is just that the all-clumped-together look now feels a little cluttered and, dare one say it, old-fashioned. Today, there may be a beautiful antique table or chairs perhaps, and when a traditional kitchen is already in situ, it is often brought up to date with small, telling additions, such as contemporary light fittings or seating. Country kitchens today are certainly informal, and perhaps not as hard-edged and sleek as they might be in a city, but they are very much fit for purpose – easy to use and, importantly, easy to keep clean. They often have within them, or very close to hand, a large family table where food preparation and eating take place, and chairs that are easily moved around the larger space. The working area may be designed around one or two walls, or it may have a free-standing counter or island unit. Although natural materials, particularly wood and stone, are deservedly popular in this type of country kitchen, metal and glass are also often brought into play. But whatever the material and design of the modern country kitchen, in one respect it is like every other room in a country house – designed to connect, in every respect, as closely as possible with the closer and greater outdoors beyond.

This page *There is a simplicity about this dining room that belies the thought that has gone into its design. Nothing is overstated – from the lightly sealed wooden-board floor to the wood- and metal-framed windows and doors, every proportion is right.*

BY APPOINTMENT TO HER MAJESTY QUEEN ELIZABETH II
TEA AND COFFEE MERCHANTS R. TWINING & CO. LTD.

TWININGS
OF LONDON

**IRISH
BREAKFAST
TEA**

PRINTED & PAINTED BY
WELLMAN & COMPANY LIMITED,
CANGGU, BALI.

BY APPOINTMENT TO HER MAJESTY QUEEN ELIZABETH II
TEA AND COFFEE MERCHANTS R. TWINING & CO. LTD.

TWININGS
OF LONDON

**EARL
GREY
TEA**

PRINTED & PAINTED BY
WELLMAN & COMPANY LIMITED,
CANGGU, BALI.

Outdoor Living

Surely it must be true that one of the main reasons for living in the country – particularly if it is somewhere that is used mostly at the weekends and for holidays – is to be able to enjoy the outdoors as much as possible.

It follows that there must be areas outside, both near to and far from the house, where you can eat, drink, sit and read, walk or indeed do nothing at all – in other words places where you can live in the same way outside, in the wider landscape, as you do inside the house. It is important, therefore, that when designing both house and garden there should be no obvious cut-off point between interior and exterior, but instead a harmonious link between the man-made and the natural. Design the interior with one eye through the windows and doors, and furnish the garden with hard landscape, plants and structures that echo or complement your interior style. Blur the boundaries on both sides and the house will appear larger and the garden closer.

Right *Outside an industrial farm building that has been made into a classic holiday home and next to a large mulberry tree, a metal pergola has been installed, up which has been trained a wisteria that now gives lunchtime shade.*

Terraces and patios

A terrace – some sort of flat, hard-surfaced area – immediately outside the house is something that many find, if not essential, then definitely desirable, as it is the obvious physical link between house and garden. In landscape design terms, a terrace anchors a house architecturally, and gives it greater significance as a building. So if one is to be added, it is important that the depth of the terrace is in proportion to the height of the house; too narrow and the house will look unbalanced, too deep and the house will appear lost in its surroundings. A terrace is the first thing that is noticed when coming out of the house, so its surface is of overriding importance; it may be

paved or flagged, it may be gravelled or made with wooden decking, but whatever surface is chosen it should not only be pleasing to the eye, but also complement the materials of the building it frames. Since a terrace acts as a stepping stone, so to speak, between the house and the land beyond, it is the obvious place for a table and chairs, as well as easy chairs for relaxing. As far as the style of garden furniture goes, there is no need to have everything matching, either in design or material; just as inside the house, the important consideration is that what you have should work together – and that there should not be too much clutter; as ever, simplicity is always the best look.

Below left *A decked terrace adds an extra dimension, as well as extra outdoor space. Where space permits, deep is preferable to shallow, particularly if there is the possibility of making use of the consequent sheltered area below.*

Below *Giving both shade and a dappled light as well as a flow of air from above, split cane makes a natural and attractive covering for a pergola, particularly one constructed on a terrace of stone.*

Opposite *Crazy paving has somewhat fallen out of favour in the last ten years, but it has an eccentric charm, accentuated here by small tables that resemble jigsaw pieces and irregular canvas-covered chairs.*

This page *The perfect outdoor eating place: a sturdy shelter with wooden beams and dried rushes woven together to provide a long, light and airy space. Electricity has been fed in so that long lunches and suppers can be taken at the rustic refectory table set with benches and log stools.*

Light and shade

When the subject of a book is modern country houses, mainly used for relaxation, the question of light and shade in a garden is obviously one of major importance. Even if a garden is in northern Europe, protection from the sun will be needed in high summer. These are the practical considerations; the aesthetic argument is that areas of shade give depth and balance to a garden, taking the eye beyond one point towards another further on. The shade might be as simple as one or two existing, wide-branched trees, beneath which a table and chair are invitingly placed, or it may be a full-blown construction, the cross beams of which are attached to a wall of the house, extending along its length and anchored with wooden posts or iron legs. Like the terrace itself, any structure that is attached should echo the proportions of the building as a natural-seeming adjunct.

The construction materials must obviously also work with the style and period of the house. Metal is all-forgiving and goes with buildings old and new. Wood is more fussy: to complement some designs it might be rough-hewn and untreated; for others it might be turned, sealed or stained. Shade-giving structures do not, of course, need to be attached to a wall of the house; equally successful are free-standing constructions, built away from the house, elsewhere in the grounds, designed either like a summer house or gazebo without walls, or as a more enclosed structure with just two or three open sides. Although traditional roofing materials such as tiles of wooden slats work well, some people – particularly in hotter climates – prefer split bamboo or cane or a wisteria or vines, through which the light is diffused and dappled.

Clockwise from top left *The easiest – if it is readily available – and most natural of shades is that of a mature, well-placed tree. Here, a very old, majestic tree is close enough to the main building to cast dappled shade over a wooden table.*

Where the sun is constantly hot and the sky blue, different areas of shade are needed for different times of day. Here, a plaster-piered open-sided room is roofed with rough, slatted pieces of wood to provide a sitting space for the heat of the day.

Not so rough and ready as it first looks, this outdoor eating space is edged with walls and pillars constructed in dry stone and hung with a roof awning of woven rush to make a room that is not a room, yet retains a semi-permanent feel.

Although it takes some years to grow large enough to be threaded through the poles of a pergola, a hardy wisteria, with first its pendant flowers and then later its distinctive seed pods, makes a fine shady covering for any garden.

Simplicity itself is this picnic table laid ready for lunch behind a rough stone wall and beneath a tree. The lightweight table and classic slatted chairs can easily be folded up and moved to another spot for another meal!

Swimming pools

As with many other supposedly modern luxuries, it was the Romans who were recorded as having the first purpose-built swimming pools. The concept of a private pool did not become popular again until the mid twentieth century when, fuelled by Hollywood, a pool became a luxury status symbol. Today, in warm climates, outdoor swimming pools are seen almost as necessities, and design – which once espoused only the traditional rectangular pool, edged with non-slip tiles and seemingly deposited in the garden wherever there was enough space – has moved on to greater heights, or rather depths. Now there are pools with undulating edges following the contours of the immediate landscape, and sometimes seemingly fed by small, rippling waterfalls; there are pools with infinity edges that seem to extend indefinitely to the horizon or beyond; and there are pools designed as narrow canals, following the precepts of classical architecture.

Today there is a wide variety of both tiles and paint colours that can be used to line or paint the interior of the pool – the choice reaches far beyond the conventional blue and turquoise, although it must be said that the colours that work best are still those that visually conjure up silent watery depths. The surrounding pool edge should be considered, too – paving, stone, tiles, concrete, decking: they should all be in harmony with both the design and the surroundings of the pool.

Above left *Particularly suitable to a hot climate is a pool into which water gushes constantly – the sound and sight are immediately cooling. This design is particularly attractive, featuring as it does a gushing pair of spouts, rather than a solitary dribble.*

Above right *Pool design today can be as contemporary as interior design and this pool, although of conventional rectangular design, is edged with bleached decking, as well as a seating area on a raised level above the water.*

Opposite *As tranquil as a natural pool, this sheet of water, designed so that it seems a very part of the countryside itself, blends perfectly into both the hard landscape of stone and paving, and the natural landscape beyond.*

Previous pages *A contemporary use for an old and magnificent barn, with its original rafters and beams, is to use it as the site of a swimming pool. This example is particularly striking as a glass wall with sliding doors has been constructed between the pool and the main reception rooms of the house.*

This page *One space is subdivided into sleeping and bathing by a rough partition wall that is deliberately built in contrast to the smooth, white outer plaster walls. On one side is the low bed, on the other a sophisticated shower and washing area.*

Bedrooms and Bathrooms

Where modern country life is concerned, the bedroom – and its corresponding bathroom – are as much about state of mind as they are decorative or design statements. They should be relaxing, obviously, and comfortable, indubitably, but they should also be open and airy, simple in concept, easy to come into and, importantly, easy to leave.

Bedrooms

Although country life is less complicated than its urban counterpart, there are certain non-negotiables that apply. Throughout the house no fuss, no trouble seems to be the order of the day. Comfort, of course, is paramount, but perhaps country comfort is not quite as complicated as city comfort – it is certainly not as busy as its urban neighbour. This seems particularly true in the case of the country bedroom versus the urban bedroom. In modern country terms, simplicity – again – is at the heart of the bedroom, whether it slides towards contemporary simplicity or veers in the direction of more classic lines. But do not confuse simplicity with austerity or lack of comfort; the bedroom must always be a pleasure to be in, otherwise what is the

point of it? The best rooms come about when each element of the modern country bedroom is considered separately and put together collectively. Patently the most important, and usually the largest, thing in a bedroom is the bed, and this should be fit for purpose, and suited to whoever is using it. There are few ornate or elaborate beds in the modern country house; quite rightly, the emphasis is on plain lines – a divan rather than a heavily upholstered bed, with only a simple head board or even none at all. Space is used ingeniously – a shelf here, a chest there; heavy pieces of storage are nowhere to be seen – indeed, all storage is kept to the absolute bare minimum. Also kept to a minimum are window hangings: curtains are rarely to be seen at country windows. Instead there may be internal or external shutters or blinds – neat, tidy pieces of material, usually in

Opposite *The sloping roof eaves and the resultant angled lines of the room have been cleverly utilized here to make a compact but comfortable sleeping area. Unlined curtains add softness to the space, and the bedhead-cum-shelves hold all necessities.*

Above *Against a sealed stone wall, a room beneath the roof is part bedroom, part bathroom. The softer decor of the bedroom has been carried over into the bathroom by using curtains under the washstand rather than cupboard doors.*

neutral colours, that fold unobtrusively into the frame of the window. Floors, too, are usually pretty bare. Wide wooden boards work well – cool in summer and warm underfoot in colder weather. Other popular options include polished cement – sometimes lightly tinted – as well as terracotta tiles or stone. These floors are often semi-covered with rugs, but rarely of the heavy Oriental variety. Country rugs are relatively light in weight and light in texture – which makes them easy to clean and easy to move. Like in every other room in the modern country house, wall colour in the bedroom is mostly noticeable by its absence; pale colours abound, usually neutrals, but sometimes also subtle tints that reflect the colours of the countryside.

Opposite *A simple bedroom, which could have been austere, but is instead a soothing compact haven, brought together by the neutral colours and tones, as well as the materials – wood, wood and wood.*

Above left *In a stone-walled bedroom that could be severe in appearance, a fabric-covered wall behind the bed coupled with a soft fabric corona above and floor-length linen bed hangings counteract the stony look.*

Above *A low ceiling beneath the eaves can work well in a bedroom as long as everything is proportioned accordingly. The bed here is at floor level, as is the bedside table; only the bedhead is of normal height.*

Opposite top left *Suitably wintry and warm, this chalet bedroom is designed to work with the wood-boarded and beamed wall behind. A goatskin covers the headboard, and the bed covers are also suitably warm in tone.*

Opposite top right *Simplicity is the key for holiday bedrooms – they are not rooms to linger in. Woven straw dishes are the only decoration here, other than the view outside the window.*

Opposite bottom *At the top of the house, huge supporting beams are decoration enough in this room. The sleeping area is divided from the bathroom by a low partition wall; all other furniture is kept to a stylish minimum.*

Right *This room is enclosed by wood, yet the effect is not claustrophobic, rather cosy and warm. Hung against a painted plaster wall, the distressed wooden boards have had different-sized circles cut out at random to create a simple design, very pleasing to the eye.*

Bathrooms

Historically, domestic washing arrangements in Europe (post-Roman Empire, needless to say) always veered towards the basic – a hundred years ago, or even less, in most countries a basin and ewer sufficed, with a portable bath to be set down in front of the fire when needed. Rare was the free-standing bath, and rarer still a comfortable lavatory; this essential convenience was often outside the house, or inside, in a small, rather smelly space of its own. The concept of luxury, or even comfort, was not part of the everyday ablutionary process. But bathrooms have come a long way since then, both in the city and the countryside. Today in a modern country house, whether converted, renovated or built from scratch, there is a new aesthetic that combines a studied simplicity with a certain type of sophisticated design. Natural materials abound – there's not much plastic to be seen in these clean havens. The basin and ewer on the washstand are long gone – the basin is now plumbed in, albeit often into a top based on the traditional stand. It might be in the bedroom – indeed, the whole bathroom might be in the bedroom, separated from the sleeping area by only a partition wall – or it might be in a dedicated room along with a bath and the all-important shower. The shower, like the rest of the bathroom, fits into a look that is an interesting mix of the traditional combined with technological innovations. It is unsurprising, perhaps, that showers now figure so strongly: they are economical to run, low on water consumption and perfect on a hot day. They are also extremely versatile: the old idea of the too-small-to-turn shower stall is long gone. Instead, there are full-blown wet rooms, as well as showers tucked into awkward corners and just separated from the rest of the bathroom by a low wall, often draining directly away through tiles or stone floors – for the floor of the bathroom will nearly always be made of natural materials.

Opposite *A bathroom so simple that it looks as if it might just have been dropped into place yesterday. A free-standing bath, two ladder towel rails leaning against the wall and a polished cement floor are all that's needed.*

Above right *Skilfully designed to look as though two bowls have just been left on a wooden table, in reality the basins are plumbed below the table, with the innards hidden by a heavy curtain. An inexpensive and stylish look.*

Below right *A small bathroom hidden in a corner at the top of the house, making the most of an awkward space. Separate free-standing basins sit on a washstand-style wooden cupboard, inside which all necessities can be stored.*

Opposite top left *A hot bath is both a necessity and a luxury in a mountain house, and this bathroom leading from the bedroom is more than fit for purpose. The bath edging, which extends beyond the bath itself, becomes a useful shelf for more than soap.*

Opposite top right *A slate floor grounds a traditional bathroom complete with commodious bath and basins. Roman blinds that fold up neatly away from the bath edge allow privacy and warmth when required.*

Opposite below *This bathroom is a mish-mash of styles and quirky pieces. An industrial locker cupboard, painted matt black, holds the towels; a comfortable antique armchair, upholstered in charcoal fabric, and an up-to-date basin and storage unit complete the look.*

Right *This is a simple and brilliantly effective way to put a shower into an unused corner. A wooden plank wall (note the hooks outside for towels and bathrobes) partitions off a shower head, which drains directly into an outlet set into the old stone-slab floor.*

Previous pages *What could be more uplifting than to shower each morning in a place where glass walls surround you and you can look out over the sea beyond? As cool and calm as the view, this bathroom has been designed for practicality as well as style.*

Left *A veritable outdoor spa, with mosaic tiles surrounding swan-like showers, and an inviting whirlpool pool. Wooden decking is a contrast to the tiles, as are the wooden walls that enclose the area.*

Index

Photographers' Credits

Amiand, Francis (architect Frédéric Lebard, stylist Gilles Dallière)
p 80, 83, 176, 188, 218/219

Clapot, Julien (architect Jean-Baptiste Barache and Silhem Lamine, stylist Agnès Zamboni)
p 20 (above right)

Delafraye, Fabienne
p 21 (architect David Juet of Atelier Kenenso, stylist Thibault de Maillard)
p 59, 93, 117, 130, 134 (architect Jacques Moussafir, stylist Thibault de Maillard)

Ducout, Frédéric (stylist Caroline Amiel)
p 56/57, 62, 66

Dugied, Christophe
p 54, 72, 73, 74, 75, 122 (above right), 132, 213 (below right) (architect Wouter Lucas Andries, stylist Catherine Cornille)
p 83, 142 (stylist Coco Jobard)
p 124, 129, 172, 173, 174, 214 (above left and right) (architect Bernard De Clercq, stylist Christine Lippens)
p 62 (above right), 96, 97, 98, 99 (architect Jean-Philippe Nuel, stylist Jérôme Aumont)

Font, Albert (architect Andrés Jaque, stylist Françoise Lefébure)
p 135, 166, 167, 168, 169, 216/217

Goudier, François (architect Catherine Brichard, stylist Marie Audhuy)
p 138, 143, 156/157, 158/159, 178

d'Hérouville Éric
p 31, 38, 39, 40, 41, 104, 108 (architect Martin Dauner, stylist Sophie Chauvain-Chiotti)
p 10, 17, 34, 35, 36/37, 121, 122 (above left), 126 (below left), 142 (architect Devanthéry & Lamunière, stylist Marie-Maud Levron)
p 92, 95, 113, 131 (architect Seth Stein, stylist Marie-Maud Levron)
p 110, 123 (above left), 184/185 (stylist Marie-Maud Levron)
p 100, 101, 102, 103 (architect Delphine Bouchet, stylist Marie-Maud Levron)

Meurant, Alexandra (architect Henri Blanchot, stylist Sophie Maillot-Juillet)
p 49, 58 (above right), 170/171 and back endpaper

Millet, Nicolas
p 7, 30, 186, 187, 210 (above left) (architect Florine Burger, stylist Julie Daurel)
p 12/13, 14 (below left), 16, 113 (above right), 127, 179, 183, 198 (above left), 199 (below left), 210 (above right) (architect Gilles Terrazzoni, stylist Julie Daurel)

del Olmo, Henri
p 19, 20/21, 66, 67, 68/69, 70, 71, 132, 192/193, 198 (below right) (interior designer Annick Lestrohan, stylist Françoise Lefébure)
p 14/15 (below centre), 18 (below right), 128, 152/153, 182, 190/191, 194 (below right), 196/197, 210, 212 (interior designer Sarah Lavoine, stylist Monique Duveau)
p 33, 139, 160, 161, 162/163, 164, 165, 177 (above), 204/205, 206 (architect Marianne Sidler, stylist Françoise Lefébure)

Palisse, Jean-Marc
p 15, 48 (architect Jean Béraud, stylist Cécilia Blachas)
p 32 (interior designer Angélique Buisson, stylist Agnès Benoit)
p 136 (architect Thomas Vidalenc)

Planells, Pere (architect Pascal Cheik Djavadi, stylist Françoise Lefébure)
p 1,15, 42/43, 44, 45

Potignon, Alain
p 20 (below right) (architect Raymond Marcus, stylist Phuong Pfeufer)
p 154 (above right) (stylist Marie-Maud Levron)

Rinuccini, Arnaud (architect Nicolas Vernoux-Thélot, interior designer Christian Signorel, stylist Jérôme Aumont)
p 59, 63, 64, 131 (above right), 142 (above right), 177 (below), 202/203

Rouffio, Christophe (architect Morten Brusk Petersen, interior design Modern Living, stylist Marie Radot)
p 76, 77, 78, 79

Siraudeau, Sebastien
p 22/23, 24/25, 118 (below right), 154 (above left), 208, 209, 213 (above right)

Suet, Bruno (architect Renaud Piérard, stylist Françoise Lefébure)
p 14 (above left), 107, 109, 112, 195, 198 (below left), 201, 224 and front endpaper

Tosi, Nicolas (interior designer Candice de Saint Sauveur, stylist Monique Duveau)
p 58 (above left), 88, 89, 90/91, 116, 214 (below left)

Touillon, Bernard
p 46, 47, 120 (above right) (interior designer Raffaele Curi, stylist Cécile Valarelli)
p 8/9, 60/61, 104/105, 126, 144, 145, 146, 147, 199 (architect Olivier Moureau, interior designer Romain Michel-Menière, stylist Monique Duveau, Cécile Valarelli)
p 4/5 (contents page), 81, 84, 85, 86, 87 (stylist Laurence Botta-Delannoy)
p 119, 123 (above right), 194 (below left) (architect Denis Barets, interior designer Guy Roisse, stylist Alix de Dives)
p 126 (above right), 133, 189, 200 (above right) (interior designer Gérard Faivre, stylist Laurence Botta-Delannoy)

Trillard, Gilles
p 3 (title page), 48, 50, 51, 52, 53, 125, 190/191, 211 (interior designer Frédéric Tabary, stylist Barbara Divry)
p 58 (below left), 94 (below left) (architect Olivier Flahault and Sabine LeMen, stylist Caroline Engel)

Van Spaerendock, Pia (stylist Marine Broussaud)
p 18 (below left), 26, 27, 28, 29, 120 (above left), 129 (above right), 140/141, 148/149, 150/151

Verger, Pierre Jean
p 137

Warion, Bruno (architect Philippe Commun, stylist Stephanie Boiteux Gallard)
p 2, 106/107, 111, 114/115, 118, 155, 175, 200, 207, 215

Acknowledgements

It is always a pleasure to do a book with Jacqui Small and her team, and this book was no exception. My thanks go to Jacqui herself, editor Jo Copestick and to designer Sarah Rock for her cool, clean design, which perfectly reflects the contemporary mood of the book. My particular thanks, though, go to Sian Parkhouse who, in my – now quite wide, and sometimes rather frustrating – experience of book editors, is a blooming marvel. Serene, patient and very efficient in a behind-the-scenes, unobtrusive way, she is a pleasure to do business with – particularly during the always arduous, and sometimes stressful, business of writing and putting together a complicated book such as this.